# THE ECLECTIC CURRICULUM IN AMERICAN MUSIC EDUCATION: CONTRIBUTIONS OF DALCROZE, KODALY, AND ORFF

BETH LANDIS
POLLY CARDER

Copyright © 1972
Music Educators National Conference

Library of Congress Catalog Card Number 72-83395

Music Educators National Conference
1201 Sixteenth Street N.W., Washington, D.C. 20036

# Contents

This book was produced by the MENC publications staff. Beth Landis, MENC Director of Publications, is well known as music educator and author of textbooks for music education. Polly Carder, MENC Editorial Assistant, is an experienced music educator who recently received the Ed.D. degree from the University of Maryland. In view of the present widespread interest in the instructional plans of Dalcroze, Kodaly, and Orff, the MENC Publications Planning Committee is pleased to make the book available. It is hoped that both the potential and the limitations for use of these European methods in the American curriculum will become apparent.

We are especially indebted to four persons who read various sections of the book and gave valuable suggestions that were incorporated in the book:

Hilda M. Schuster, Director
The Dalcroze School of Music, New York City

Denise Bacon, Musical and Educational Director
Kodaly Musical Training Institute, Wellesley, Massachusetts

Katinka Scipiades Daniel, Leader in Kodaly Instruction
Santa Barbara, California

Arnold E. Burkart, Executive Secretary
American Orff-Schulwerk Association, Muncie, Indiana

Many publishers gave permission for use of quotations and articles and others allowed photo reproduction of entire pages of their publications. The book is enriched by these contributions. Photographs were provided by the readers named above, by Brunhilde Dorsch, and by publishers, to whom we express appreciation.

ROBERT BAYS, Chairman
Publications Planning Committee

# PART ONE

# 1 THREE DISTINCTIVE APPROACHES

# INTRODUCTION

American music education is and always has been highly eclectic. The strong style and content that can be recognized and identified as "American" has as its chief characteristic purposeful selection from available ideas. From Lowell Mason's course of musical instruction based on theories of Pestalozzi (who in turn had been influenced by Rousseau), to the present complex music curriculums in schools and universities, Americans have seen fit to adopt or adapt and develop any useful educational concept.

In recent years, three European musical doctrines have permeated practice in American schools: those of Emile Jaques-Dalcroze, Zoltan Kodaly, and Carl Orff. The word doctrines seems inadequate to describe the ideas of these men, yet the ideas were not presented as fully sufficient and independent methods, even by their creators. American music education, at every age level, embraces vocal and instrumental performance, listening and analysis, experimentation, improvisation, and composition. It is based on literature that spreads from the latest in American popular music back through medieval plainsong, and from sounds of the Chinese *sho* to those of the synthesizer. In such a curriculum no one of the doctrines, nor all three together, can form a complete course of study. But as an approach, each doctrine, or adaptations of it, can contribute immeasurably to the complete or comprehensive American ideal.

The three doctrines are in some ways related, although each has its own purposes and practices. Both Kodaly and Orff consciously learned from Dalcroze; Carl Orff has said that he recognizes the interrelationship of his instructional philosophy with that of Kodaly; Kodaly once visited the Orff Institute in Salzburg and purchased a set of the special instruments designed for the *Schulwerk*. Leaders of the Orff and Kodaly movements visit each other in Europe and in the United States for interchange of ideas, and they successfully combine the two methods in workshops. All three men knew the usual plans of music teaching in their times, and discerning the weaknesses, tried to overcome them. Neither man created his system out of thin air. Each used the musical and educational principles he felt to be most useful in accomplishing his purposes and developing his own plan. The hand signs that are basic to Kodaly's plan of teaching note reading, he adopted after he observed music teaching in England and saw the signs being used in the Tonic Sol-Fa College founded by Curwen. The chant and movement that are such useful and attractive components of Orff's teaching appeared first in the Dalcroze school.

The basic ideas on which successful teaching methods are built seldom are entirely new, nor do good ideas, as a rule, come to only one person. Change and progress in education often are based on ideas whose time has come. The fact that an idea has recurred again and again in educational practice indicates that it is worthy of our consideration. New and different approaches to persistent problems may result from creative application of an old idea. Furthermore, when musicians and thinkers of the stature of Emile Jaques-Dalcroze, Zoltan Kodaly, and Carl Orff have developed systems they believe to be sound, educators naturally must take note of them.

One purpose of this book is to delineate as clearly and succinctly as possible the plan devised by each of the three musician-educators. The second purpose is to point out ways in which elements of the plans can be adapted to enrich and make more efficient the music teaching and learning in American schools. The individual teacher always has carried an important responsibility for awareness of current trends in educational thought, for making judgments of the values of these trends, and for putting into practice those procedures he believes best suited to his students. Referring again to Lowell Mason, whose work in public school music began in 1837, one might be surprised to read these statements from his "Elements of Vocal Music."

It is taken for granted in the following synopsis that the teacher is familiar with his work, or that he knows how to teach; pedagogic directions have therefore been mostly omitted; not even the questions common in such elementary works have been inserted, on the supposition that the man who is qualified to teach will be able to ask his own questions. The practical exercises, too, must be regarded as specimens; for as the good teacher of arithmetic does not rely exclusively upon his text book, but often gives out original or extemporaneous questions, growing out of the immediate circumstances by which he is surrounded, so the good music teacher will write lessons impromptu. . . . There is a freshness and lively interest in such lessons that cannot be reached by the most carefully prepared book exercises. . . . The best teacher will not be confined to any particular previously laid out plan, but will from the different methods make out one of his own; not indeed one that is stereotyped and unalterable, but one that he may modify and adapt to the varying wants and circumstances of his different classes.[1]

It hardly seems necessary to rephrase Mason's statement for today's teacher. The need for awareness and application of all that can be known is greater than ever before. Modern pluralistic American society and the complexities of plans for school organization and grouping, coupled with the diverse innate natures and modes of learning of the individuals we teach, require, without doubt, every tool available to us.

---

[1] Lowell Mason, "Elements of Vocal Music."

# THE APPROACH OF EMILE JAQUES-DALCROZE

Emile Jaques-Dalcroze formulated his approach to music education earlier than Kodaly or Orff, yet his instructional principles and procedures are particularly appropriate for today's music classes. During a long and varied teaching career that began in 1891, Dalcroze met many of the same problems that confront music educators today. The subject was divided into isolated compartments such as sightsinging, form, and harmony without emphasis on the interdependence of these studies. There was a need for development of musicianship. Dalcroze was frustrated by the fact that his students experienced difficulty in performing correct rhythms even though in ordinary physical movements they showed excellent rhythm. Out of these and similar observations grew one of the most unusual and influential methods in the history of music education, a method based on the idea that the source of musical rhythm is the natural locomotor rhythms of the human body. Today many people refer to the entire method as Eurhythmics, but the term used in that way is misleading. In a complete course of Dalcroze training, the studies that usually comprise a college music major's curriculum are included. Among them are singing, ear training, harmony, counterpoint, form, music history, applied music, and participation in vocal and instrumental ensembles.

Courtesy Hilda M. Schuster, Dalcroze School of Music, New York City.

Music instruction in the Dalcroze method involves three areas of study: *solfege*, aimed at developing an acute ear for sound; improvisation, for developing the capacity for free invention; and eurhythmics, to give students a feeling for musical rhythm by means of bodily movement.

Eurhythmics, the only entirely new subject in the Dalcroze method, has always been associated with the name of Dalcroze, and is frequently considered as the sole area of study in his method. The areas of *solfege* and improvisation were incorporated by Dalcroze in his teaching of theory and harmony, however, before eurhythmics was developed and are considered of equal importance in Dalcroze training.[1]

Today we are urged to make schools more humanistic—to provide for the fullest awareness of self and for the fulfillment of each person's potential. The Dalcroze approach contributes to self-understanding by helping a person to become aware of and to develop the expressive possibilities of his body. The range of feeling inspired by music is recognized and developed. Mental processes are sharpened and coordinated with physical and emotional processes. A person develops a new expressive dimension that goes beyond the usual verbal one. Self-development grows out of this self-awareness and understanding. In Dalcroze classes, the individual acquires skills that enable him to express himself fully and unselfconsciously. In a general philosophy such as that of the contemporary practical philosopher Abraham Maslow, self-actualization is described as the state in which a person performs toward the extent of his potential, is self-motivated and inner directed without need for extrinsic stimulus. Eurhythmics fulfills these goals of today, for it is an experience in which the person becomes absorbed in musical sound and the expressive possibilities of movement, and performs beyond his own expectations. He learns to use his body as easily as his voice. In this experience individuality is valued and encouraged. Dalcroze instruction assumes that the satisfaction that comes from a deep artistic experience has important effects upon a person.

The Dalcroze method is in many ways the counterpart of today's thrust toward education for comprehensive musicianship. In recent years, comprehensive musicianship courses have sought to synthesize and relate experiences in composition, performance, analytical listening, and theory. Dalcroze saw the weakness in separation of musical studies. He planned for the development of a kind of musicianship that included not only accurate performance of the musical score, but a sensitive expression of all the interpreti.e elements of the music: dynamics, phrasing, nuances, and shading.

It is apparent from Dalcroze's observations that compartmentalism, especially in higher education, is no new phenomenon. Piano courses were not collated with those in harmony, nor those in harmony with those dealing with the history of music, nor was the history of music applied to a study of the general history of peoples and individuals. There was no cohesion in the tuition of syllabuses, although they were profuse in their subject matter, and each professor was confined to his own narrow domain, having little contact with his colleagues who specialized in other branches of musical science.[2]

In the time of Dalcroze and long afterward, education by principle without practice was common.

When he asked his students to write down chords during their harmony classes he discovered that they were not really hearing what they had written, and that for most of them harmony was simply a matter of mathematics. It became clear to him that the traditional method of training musicians concentrated on the intellect to the detriment of the senses, and failed to give students a valid *experience* of the basic elements of music sufficiently early in their studies.

He also noticed that although his students learnt to play their instruments and sing songs accurately, they did not think of their performance as a means of self-expression. . . . Technique had become an end in itself.[3]

Dalcroze formulated his whole approach to music education on synthesis of theoretical knowledge and skills and application of them. Sensory and intellectual experiences are fused. He believed that the skills and understandings of the least and most accomplished musician are built on active involvement in musical experience.

Present-day emphasis on teaching concepts of musical elements was anticipated by Dalcroze. In his method, musical elements are encountered in numerous successive and concurrent experiences that lead to genuine understanding and skill. The element of rhythm is of first importance in early experiences. Dynamic and tempo changes are heard and felt in the first lessons. Pitch, texture, and other elements are soon treated as a part of the sound palette. In ear training and dictation exercises, all elements are studied, and they are given further attention in improvisation exercises at the piano. Through movement, students can experience both the symmetry and the pull of the musical phrase. Qualities of rising and falling, greater and lesser intensity, and "towardness" can be effectively learned by students who are responding physically to music as they hear it.

Dalcroze gave particular attention to the sequence of the student's musical experiences. He was especially concerned that instrumental study should not begin before ear training and rhythmic movement. He said, "I contend that an amateur should learn music before he touches the piano," and again, "It is veritable nonsense to have the child begin the study of instrumental music before he has manifested, either naturally or by training, some knowledge of rhythm and tone."[4] Contemporary writers in music education often have noted that a child's experiences with an instrument should be preceded by and concurrent with rich and varied experiences in listening, singing, dancing, and composing.

In the various organizational schemes of contemporary education, with new plans for grouping and scheduling and new demands for freedom and deep involvement, the Dalcroze approach to the study of music has much to offer. Groups of different numbers of students are not a detriment in this system, and in fact may be advantageous. Rhythmic movement lends itself to large and small groups, open spaces, and variable-length class periods. Tremendous impetus in rhythmic movement can come from large groups of students experiencing musical sounds together, according to authorities in Dalcroze work. Large and small spaces can be used advantageously. Activities in solfege and piano improvisation can be done in small groups. Some of the study of theory and harmony can be done through individualized instruction. Older and younger students can work together profitably and with pleasure. Many of today's inner city children do not communicate well in classroom situations because their vocabularies are limited and perhaps very different from the teacher's vocabulary. A teacher who understands Dalcroze principles can adapt them to such children. Through listening to music and experiencing it in movement, the children can develop healthy self-concepts, and their inner feelings can be explored, expressed, and shaped.

Observers are surprised to see how few textbooks are used by students of the Dalcroze system at all levels, from the smallest children to those preparing to teach the method. Of course some of the areas of study, such as music history and literature, are largely dependent on textbook materials; but a great many principles of music theory, form, and vocal technique are learned through participation. Exercises are often notated on chalkboards by the teacher or the students according to the purpose of the exercise. Furthermore, Dalcroze said that teachers cannot learn his system of musical instruction from books and musical scores—that participation in training classes is the only effective way of learning the subject. Important to the Dalcroze plan is its stress on the feelings of the student in response to music, and on the channeling of these feelings into expression. Those who have studied the Dalcroze method say that it can no more be learned by reading about it than swimming can be. They think that personal experience is the only way of learning this system. The ideas must be tried to be evaluated. Individuality is stressed, and the teacher who adopts ideas from the method must trust his own individuality and find ways to apply the principles in his own way to his teaching. One qualification of the teacher that Dalcroze had a great deal to say about is ability to improvise at the piano.

The reader must remember that all the music is improvised. From the very nature of the exercises it is impossible to use written music. M. Jaques-Dalcroze has composed, in addition to his *Action Songs* for children, music which may be used in plastic exercises and these are occasionally employed by the teacher; but for the most part the music must be created spontaneously. That is why the method in its complete form lays so much stress on ear-training and improvisation; and that is also why those who profess to be Dalcroze teachers after a few lessons in rhythmic movement can only offer the husk of this training. The whole kernel is lacking—the understanding of musical harmony, the ability to improvise rhythms illustrative of the various musical principles and laws, and worst lack of all the ability to improvise exercises by combining the elements of several already given.[5]

The teacher's ability to improvise at the piano is absolutely essential if the method is to be used as Dalcroze intended. This includes the ability to create a different "movement feeling" for each exercise since students learn to let music move them in whole-body responses. The music provided must also be completely appropriate to the idea being taught, whether that idea is crescendo, or largo, or the rise and fall of a melodic phrase.

# RHYTHMIC MOVEMENT

Although the Dalcroze method consists of three main branches: eurhythmics (rhythmic movement), solfege, and piano improvisation, the basic approach is the experience of rhythm through body movement, and this experience dominates the early lessons. Dalcroze first used rhythmic movement as a mode of instruction in solfege classes and in private lessons. Today in Dalcroze training, eurhythmics is used in all classes to teach practically every aspect of music. Dalcroze believed that rhythm is the fundamental, motivating force in all the arts, especially in music. He recognized that human life is characterized by rhythms such as those of the heartbeat and of breathing. He based his teaching on the principle that musical rhythms parallel the rhythms of life. In music, rhythm is actually motion: the animating factor that gives continuity and impetus to sounds. All types of motion found in music are studied through rhythmic movement. Even exercises in solfege and improvisation are introduced through rhythm and are done in rhythm. Standard classroom percussion instruments, such as sticks, triangles, tambourines, sand blocks, and small drums are used extensively in classes for adults as well as children. Their function is to extend the possibilities of muscular response to music.

Of the three elements he found in music—sound, rhythm and dynamics, the last two depended entirely on movement and had their counterpart in our muscular systems. Changes of tempo (allegro, andante, etc.,) and dynamics (forte, piano, crescendo, diminuendo) could be expressed by our bodies, and the intensity of our musical feelings depended on the intensity of our physical sensations.[6]

With rhythmic movement as the basic mode of instruction, musical concepts are internalized. Dalcroze planned to teach the elements—rhythm, melody, harmony, dynamics, form, and phrasing—through leading his students to experience these things in movement. He believed that immediate physical response—realizing the music as it is heard—is essential to the comprehension of a musical idea. Rhythmic movement is the means by which all the different kinds of movement in music, such as the flow of melody, the shifting of harmony, the phrase that is a musical equivalent of the human breath, can be known. In the words of Dalcroze:

It is my object, after endeavoring to train the pupil's ear, to awaken in him, by means of special gymnastics, the sense of his personal body-rhythm, and to induce him to give metrical order to the spontaneous manifestations of his physical nature. Sound rhythms had to be stepped, or obtained by gestures; it was also necessary to find a system of notation capable of measuring the slightest nuances of duration, so as to respond to both the demands of the music and to the bodily needs of the individual.[7]

In his writings, Dalcroze used the term sound to mean a combination of pitch, timbre, and dynamics. He seemed to include in this term all aspects of musical tone except rhythm. The word gymnastics he used to mean rhythmic movement. He found it an unsatisfactory term when he first used it, and certainly today it does not convey the essential meaning of the method. The word rhythm he used to mean movement in music. In its narrow sense, this means the *takt* or measure beat and the subdivisions of that beat. It includes the concepts of melodic rhythm, harmonic rhythm, word rhythms in vocal music, and the rhythm patterns of accompaniment figures. In a wider sense it includes dynamic intensity, the balance of equal and unequal phrases, and elements of the formal structure of a composition that give it drive, impetus, or motion. Students of the Dalcroze method are taught that rhythm is really motion, and they become aware of all the ways in which motion is evident in music.

In typical Dalcroze classes, a musical concept such as accelerando is built gradually. It may begin with an imaginative idea such as the representation of a person or object in the act of gaining speed. This movement is done first without music; it should be familiar movement from daily life. Then the student listens to music in which accelerando is unmistakable, and discovers movement that corresponds with what he has just done. Then he is ready to synchronize his movement spontaneously with appropriate music. Recognition of the term accelerando follows. Other musical concepts are built in the same way. In a later lesson the student will see the written symbol for accelerando, respond with muscular sensations, use the idea in notation and in improvisation. A basic principle of this method is that time, space, and energy are interrelated, as tempo, dynamics, and other elements in music are interrelated. By synchronizing his movements with music as he hears it, the student experiences these interrelationships. He analyzes simultaneous elements and successive musical events by realizing them in movement. For example, by walking on tiptoe, with steps becoming longer and longer, stretching forward and upward while bringing more of the foot down with each successive step, making larger and larger movements, students "realize" a crescendo.

In eurhythmics classes, students move freely with music improvised by the teacher at the piano. In bare feet and comfortable clothing, class members skip, walk, run, and leap through individual movements that are evoked by the musical sounds. Intrinsic to the process is intensive listening that is

"End of the Phrase," preprimary children in Dalcroze Eurhythmics class, Duquesne University, Pittsburgh. Courtesy Brunhilde E. Dorsch, teacher.

natural since the physical response depends on it. In general, mechanical and stereotyped steps and movements are avoided. The spontaneous quality of the movement is derived from the fact that the music is being created while students listen. The music will be different for each successive exercise, and responses cannot be anticipated.

A striking Phenomenon in lessons in eurhythmics is the extreme diversity of individual movements on the part of those who do the same exercises together, to the same music. In other words, there are great differences of interpretation of the same musical rhythms by different persons. This variety corresponds exactly to the personal characteristics of the various pupils, and it may be interesting to see why this individual factor, so striking in our classes, is absent in gymnastic or military exercises where hundreds of individuals do the same movement in the same way. The reason is that the gestures of soldiers or gymnasts are an end in themselves, whereas those of our pupils are the manifestation of their higher will imposing certain rhythms on their bodily movements. Exercises in athletics or drill aim at a purely material object, whereas we endeavor to produce a common outward expression of individual emotions. Here rhythm is the link between mind and senses, and this to such a degree that each pupil speedily rejects the current opinion which looks upon the body as inferior to the mind. He quickly comes to regard his body as an instrument of incomparable delicacy, susceptible of the noblest and the most artistic expression.[8]

Individuality of movement is encouraged. Each student has natural, characteristic movements and styles of moving that give a unique quality to his work. Dalcroze recognized this fact and capitalized on it. Each student feels the music in the deepest sense. He expresses it unselfconsciously with his entire body. Dalcroze believed that when this idea is carried to its logical extreme, the body will become a musical instrument. The student will hear, analyze, internalize, and become one with the music.

The basic rhythms played at the piano by the teacher are those that match natural rhythms of human movement, such as walking, running, skipping, and swinging. A teacher often asks a student to begin a specific movement and, watching the tempo and intensity of the response, plays in that tempo and at that dynamic level. There is a natural development from simple basic movements to complex movement in which students may interpret a canon, or several musical elements simultaneously. As a musical instrument, the body is called upon to perform in complex ways, often with the arms interpreting one pattern, the feet another, and other parts of the body others. For example, the arms may conduct in 4/4 meter while the feet move with a syncopated rhythmic pattern and the head nods on specified beats. In another exercise the teacher plays one measure before the students begin to move. The students then respond to the first measure as they listen to the second and so on through the composition. In a different exercise, students speak or sing one pattern of rhythm with a text and perform a different pattern in movement. Students learn to expect sudden change in the music and to respond at once. The change may be in tempo, dynamics, or meter. For example, the change may consist of a contrasting style of music, or of small variations on a single element. The student responds instantly and in good form to what he hears. A result of such exercises is ability to respond sensitively to the most refined nuances in music. Students express the rise and fall of phrases, intricate shading of timbre, tempo, and dynamics in addition to basic musical elements. This is what Dalcroze meant when he spoke of the body as a musical instrument. An observer has the interesting experience of *seeing* people *feel* music. A teacher, watching students respond to music in this way, is concerned entirely with movement as evidence of the students' comprehension of musical elements. The students are not performing for others, but are internalizing musical concepts through physical experience.

In Europe in the late nineteenth century, at the time Dalcroze conceived of rhythmic movement as a form of music education, there was a growing interest in gymnastics and in new forms of dance. A freer kind of interpretive dance was developing in opposition to the stereotyped, mannered style of the classical ballet. In this new form called modern dance, the Americans Isadora Duncan, Ted Shawn, and Ruth St. Denis became leaders. Dalcroze insisted that he was not a teacher of the dance, and that all his innovations in rhythmic movement were made for the sole purpose of teaching music. Yet others considered that he made a great contribution to the art of the dance. He greatly increased the possibilities of gesture by having people experiment with space, moving different parts of their bodies in different spatial planes. The intense concentration on listening to music and the correlation of movement with music were naturally beneficial to dancers. Mary Wigman studied with Dalcroze for several years and then, using some of the principles he taught, built a most successful career as a dancer. Ted Shawn and Ruth St. Denis directed that the members of their troupe, the Denishawn dancers, study the Dalcroze work; in this group were Martha Graham and Doris Humphries. Among those who explored the possibilities of Dalcroze's principles for choreography were Vaslav Nijinsky and George Balanchine. Leading teachers of the Dalcroze method today, however, reiterate the statement of the originator: "We are teaching music, not the dance." While he was teaching a solfege class, about 1895, Dalcroze observed some inadequacies in the singing. At this time, he devised exercises to be done in a sitting position, with arms and hands alone, to improve the feeling for melodic line. In 1902 he directed that whole-body movements be done. He also insisted that students have bare feet—a practice that was absolutely shocking at the time.

# ORIGINAL EXERCISES IN RHYTHMIC MOVEMENT

After he had taught for a while using the plan of developing musical skills and understandings through rhythmic movement, Dalcroze made a written record of some of the exercises he had devised. Today these exercises, translated into English, give much less than a complete insight into the procedures used in eurhythmics classes. Dalcroze realized that when they were written the spontaneity essential to the method would be lost in writing about it. He explained that the exercises he wrote were meant for those who had studied in his classes, as reminders of some of their most productive learning experiences. Sixty-six exercises were described in *Rhythm, Music and Education,* twenty-two under the heading of "Rhythmic Movement" and the same number under each of the headings "Solfege or Aural Training" and "Pianoforte Improvisation." Ten representative exercises are quoted here from an adaptation of Dalcroze's book *The Importance of Being Rhythmic: A Study of the Principles of Dalcroze Eurhythmics Applied to General Education and to the Arts of Music, Dancing, and Acting* by Jo Pennington. They will give the reader some idea of the way in which instructional procedures in eurhythmics were described during the years when they first became known in the United States.

*Exercises in Rhythmic Movement*
In order that the reader may have some definite idea of the nature of the exercises in rhythmic movement, we shall describe those listed in the following program. This program is selected because it was given at a public demonstration lesson of eurythmics and because it gives representative exercises. These exercises are merely a sample —just such an introduction to an understanding of the Dalcroze method as an understanding of the alphabet is an introduction to the English language. They are described here merely to give a definite focus to the general principles set forth in the early part of this chapter; to show how those principles have been framed in the form of exercises.

*Exercise 1. Following the Music, Expressing Tempo and Tone Quality*
The teacher at the piano improvises music to which the pupils march (usually in a circle) beating the time with their arms (3/4, 5/8, 12/8, etc.) as an orchestra leader conducts, and stepping with their feet the note values (that is, quarter notes are indicated by normal steps, eighth notes by running steps, half notes by a step and a bend of the leg, a dotted eighth and a sixteenth by a skip, etc.). The teacher varies the expression of the playing, now increasing or decreasing the intensity of tone, now playing more slowly or more quickly; and the pupils "follow the music" literally, reproducing in their movements the exact pattern and structure of her improvisation.

*Exercise 2. Attention and Inhibition*
These two exercises of attention and inhibition are exercises in mental

control, concentration and coordination of mind and body. In (a) the pupils march to the music and at "hopp" take one step backward. As this word comes at quite irregular intervals and they have no warning of it, they must listen carefully and be ready to respond, both mentally and muscularly, the moment they hear the command. In (b) the pupils march to the music and at a signal stop and count silently the two, three, four or more beats agreed upon and then take up their march exactly on time. This is an exercise in silent counting, demanding concentration and a consciousness of the beat in the muscles as well as in the brain—a kind of training in muscular memory. It is amusing to note how unfailingly beginners take up the marching too soon, seldom too late. The tendency of the un-trained mind is to quicken the beat while the music is silent because the mind operates consciously whereas the muscles should record and retain the impression without conscious effort.

*Exercise 3. Arm Movements to Indicate Measure*
As explained in the first exercise, the movements of the arm indicate the measure of the music. They are modeled on those of the orchestra conductor. In two-four time the arms move down for the metric accent and then up for the second beat; in three-four they move down, sideways and then up; in four-four, they move down, crossed in front of the body, sideways and then up, etc.

*Exercise 4. Note Values. Syncopation*
In the exercise to demonstrate note values, the pupils march one step for each beat while the teacher plays quarter notes; two for each beat in eighth notes; three for triplets, etc. The values of whole and half notes are also represented, the half note by a step and a bend, and the whole note by a step followed by three or more movements of the leg without stepping. Exercises in syncopation require more training. The teacher plays an even tempo—say quarter notes in four-four time. The pupils at a command walk in syncopation for one measure or more—stepping either just before or just after the beat . . . anticipating the beat or retarding it. As their *feet* take steps just *off the beat,* their *arms* must continue to beat the time regularly, each movement being made *on the beat.* This exercise then is one in concentration, mental and physical control (coordination) and in the understanding of the musical principles of polyrhythm and syncopation.

*Exercise 5. Conducting*
In the exercise in conducting, one pupil takes his place before the others and conducts them just as the leader of an orchestra conducts, indicating the tempo the pupils are to take in their marching, direct-

ing crescendo and diminuendo at will, quicker and slower speeds, heaviness or lightness of feeling to be expressed in their movements, accents to be made (other than the metric accent on the first beat of each measure which is always indicated by a stamp of the foot). These accents on beats other than the first are pathetic accents. This exercise is first of all an exercise in self-control and spontaneous improvisation in rhythmic movement on the part of the "conductor"; on the part of the pupils it is the same as the first exercise of this program.

### Exercise 6. Phrasing

Everyone knows that music, like speech, is broken up into phrases. A singer pauses to take a fresh breath at the beginning of a new phrase. In movement a new phrase may be indicated in several ways: such as a change of direction of the march on the part of the whole group, or by a change from one arm to another on the part of the individual. This is an exercise in ear-training, in attention and in the creation of new ways of expressing the beginning of a phrase, that is, improvisation.

### Exercise 7. "Realization" of Rhythms

As explained in the program, to "realize" in the Dalcroze sense means to express in bodily movements all the elements of the music save sound. In this exercise the teacher plays a series of measures and the pupils, after listening to them, realize in their movements the rhythm which they have heard—expressing the note values, the meter, the shading, the quickness or slowness—they reproduce the rhythm in movement as definitely as though it were written in ordinary musical notation. In fact that is usually the next step in the exercise. This exercise combines several important elements of Dalcroze Eurythmics: ear training; the musical analysis of rhythm; memory and concentration; and the physical response necessary to the execution of the rhythm in movement.

### Exercise 8. Exercise in Canon

The teacher improvises measures in a given meter and the pupils realize the rhythm of each measure just after its execution by the teacher; that is, in canon. This exercise combines the principles of exercise 1, 2, 3, 4 and 7 and adds to it the close concentration required to listen to one measure while executing the preceding one. Everyone knows those old songs, "Scotland's Burning" and "Three Blind Mice" in which one singer begins and sings one phrase; the second singer begins later and so on. This exercise follows the same musical principle. No pupil of eurythmics will ever quail before the legendary terrors of a "Bach Fugue" who has arrived at an understanding of the principle of canon for that is the basis of the composition of a fugue.

*Exercise 9. Independence of Control*
This exercise is one in polyrhythm, the pupil expressing several rhythms at the same time. He may perhaps beat three-four time with the left arm and four-four with the right at the same time walking twelve-eight with the feet. There are many variations of this though in the beginning pupils find it sufficiently difficult to beat two with one arm and three with the other, especially since each arm must "remember" so to speak, the accent which falls on the first beat of its own measure. Another form of this exercise is to have the pupils march one measure while beating time for another; as three with the arms and four with the feet. These are worked out mathematically at first but soon the pupils learn to keep in their muscular and mental consciousnesses the pulse of the two rhythms simultaneously.

*Exercise 10. Rhythmic Counterpoint*[9]
Rhythmic counterpoint is an exercise in the appreciation of unplayed beats. The teacher improvises a short theme, let us say simply two half notes and a quarter in five-four time. The pupil, instead of stepping on the first, third and fifth beats of the measure, will do the counterpoint by stepping on the *second* and *fourth*. Or, if told to do the counterpoint in eighth notes, he will fill in every unplayed eighth note beat. This is an exercise in inhibition and in the accurate analysis of time values.

A more complicated form of exercise is the realization of theme and counterpoint simultaneously. For example, the pupils may learn a simple melody for a theme and then proceed to sing this melody while executing a rhythmic counterpoint, as a sort of accompaniment, with steps, or with gestures. This is a very interesting exercise to watch for first one hears the note played by the teacher and following it the steps taken by the pupils to fill in the measure, the whole making a sound pattern as well as a rhythmic pattern.[10]

# SOLFEGE

Dalcroze believed that the study of Solfege awakens the sense of musical pitch and tone relations and the ability to distinguish tone qualities. It develops the ability to listen, the ability to hear, and remember (tonal memory). It should develop a *consciousness of sound.* Dalcroze used the *fixed Do* syllables. . . . The earliest Solfege study begins to establish C in one's tonal memory. From C, a thorough study is made, hearing and singing the C major scale and the tonal relationships within the scale. All of this is done through the ear, through the muscular sense of singing and through hand positions designating tones of the scale—all before any writing. First the instinct, and then the intellect.[11]

Dalcroze's goal in teaching solfege was development of the capacity he called inner hearing. Through intensive application of theoretical principles in connection with movement, students acquire the ability to hear in their minds as they look at the musical score, rhythm patterns, melodic intervals, phrasing, and dynamic nuances. "Mental hearing depends on sensation and memory, so that the art of sight-reading is based on a good receptive condition, on spontaneity of mind, and on certain powers of creative imagination, for intermediate sound-images that serve as bases for reading."[12]

Solfege sessions are a part of each Dalcroze class. Students sing intervals and songs with syllables, and improvise vocally. In learning pitch relationships, students may sing one or more measures aloud, then one or more measures silently. Or, when ending one song and beginning another, students may sing the final pitch of the first song, then the beginning pitch of the second, naming the interval between them. The piano is used to test accuracy of the interval. Many times during a solfege session, students are asked to sing the syllable do, which in the European fixed-do system is always C. Students are expected to work toward acquisition of absolute pitch. Children who are not yet three years old experiment with pitch through body movement, using the space around them to explore highness and lowness. They discover first the wider differences, or the extremes in pitch. In successive lessons smaller intervals are introduced, and they respond to the direction of a melody as they hear it in ascending, descending, or repeating tones. Three-year-olds play musical games in which they match pitches and identify a specific sound whenever it is heard. Intensive listening is essential. It is assumed that a good ear can be developed, and the teaching of solfege is directed toward that end. Advanced students sightsing exercises that correspond in difficulty with those used in conservatories. All scales are sung from C to C, usually with syllables but sometimes with letters. When students need to use the movable do system outside their Dalcroze classes, it is taught in addition to fixed do. In Dalcroze's own classes, "After the class had mastered the singing of scales from 'c' to 'c,' a melody would be played and any student could be expected to identify the correct key and sing the scale from 'c' to 'c.' " [13]

Note reading usually is not the starting point in a planned sequence of musical learning. An ideal sequence begins with hearing musical sounds, includes some sort of active responses to them, and culminates in note reading and writing. This correctly suggests to children that notation is a means of storing and communicating musical ideas, and is not the heart of the subject. Many activities help to prepare children for reading notation. The youngest students listen to scale tones played at the piano and identify them by standing beside cards, numbered one through eight, that are placed in a row on the floor. Children respond to rhythm patterns they hear by marking with crayons on large pieces of paper in a kind of beginning dictation. Dots represent the shortest note values and dashes of varying lengths represent longer note values. Children choose and display cards with quarter notes or eighth notes written on them. These cards are used in various ways to identify their movements, such as walking or running. In a class of older students, a two-measure rhythm pattern is interpreted in movement, students are asked to notate it, and the relationship between the two measures is analyzed. Pairs of students play rhythms on sticks, in simple and complex patterns, striking their own or each other's sticks. The Dalcroze teaching process begins with natural movements that are a normal part of human life: walking, running, and jumping, for example. Next, students hear rhythms in music that are analogous to these physical movements. They synchronize their movements with the music as they hear it. After a number of such experiences, they are ready to observe in musical notation the rhythm patterns they have experienced. When these patterns

"Skipping in Threes" from Elsa Findlay, *Rhythm and Movement: Applications of Dalcroze Eurhythmics* (Evanston, Illinois: Summy-Birchard Company, 1971), p.68. Used by permission.

are later encountered in a musical score, students can recognize and respond to them because of physiological, as well as intellectual, associations.

The following exercises are examples of the ways in which Dalcroze himself taught melody in his classes.

A melody would be placed on the blackboard with some empty measures which the student would be expected to fill in, improvising, as he sang the melody for the first time.

Another exercise involved writing a melody on the blackboard and as the students sang it through, each phrase was erased upon completion of this initial singing. A student would then be asked to sing the entire melody by memory.[14]

In the study of harmony, Dalcroze led his students to sing arpeggiated chords from bass to soprano. A simple chord sequence such as tonic-dominant-tonic could be sung in this way, and then more complex chord sequences could be introduced. In other exercises, students were asked to name specific chords as they heard them. "In chordal singing, students were expected to shift from one part to another upon command. Chordal sequences, placed upon the blackboard, would be played by Dalcroze with certain errors which the student was expected to hear and correct. Other chordal sequences were written on the blackboard, erased as they were sung, and then sung by memory."[15]

# IMPROVISATION

One of the three basic areas of experience in the Dalcroze plan is improvisation at the piano. The goal of piano improvisation is to give the same freedom at the instrument that students have in whole-body responses to music. This freedom is developed, in part, by assigning exercises in extemporaneous playing, which are performed in a given tempo and carried out at a brisk pace that does not allow for self-consciousness or negative attitudes. For example, as children are moving freely to music improvised by the teacher, one child may be asked to move toward the piano, improvise a "flute part" in the high register or a "drum part" in the lower as the teacher continues his playing in the middle register, all without interruption of the pulse or the movement activity of the rest of the class. Small children often improvise rhythmic patterns on a single tone in descant style, while the teacher plays a sequence of chords. Through consistency of such practices, students develop improvisation skills and gain a sense of success that contributes to the creative quality of their work.

Dalcroze made improvisation an integral part of the study of music. A musical trait often found in well trained musicians of the past, this art of instantaneous (or extemporaneous) "composition" had fallen into disuse as a general tool of the musician. Dalcroze incorporated improvisation into his theoretical harmony classes by having students invent melodies or fragments of melodies as they sought to improve their interval comprehension, both singing and listening. As the students progressed, they were introduced to keyboard improvisation as a means of becoming more familiar with the harmonic structure of music.[16]

Improvisation with other instruments and with voice follows a similar pattern. In one experience students play a given measure on percussion instruments. In turn they improvise consequent measures following repetitions of the antecedent measure. Children are careful not to lose the basic beat, and no two consequent measures are alike. It is characteristic of the Dalcroze method that spoken commands or signals are given during the process of improvisation. This technique helps to develop intensive listening to all aspects of the music, but it also helps students perfect certain musical skills. For example, while the children are executing a specific rhythmic pattern with their feet, the teacher may call for a contrasting rhythm to be done with the arms.

Students were encouraged by Dalcroze to improvise their own choice of chords and chord progressions, eventually fitting these into a specific form. . . . Melodies would be improvised above these chords, with the added complications of change of meter and rhythm, and with modulations. Dance forms, scherzos, rondos, even moods were suggested as forms for improvisation. Advanced students would improvise together on two pianos, both alternating and in simultaneous performance, requiring a high level of attentive listening, sensitivity, and adjustment to each other. Vocal improvisations among three or more students were also attempted, often quite successfully.[17]

In one exercise four pitches such as C, D, E, F-sharp are given. As the teacher plays a harmonic background, students, in turn, sing an improvised rhythmic pattern of two measures using any two of the four pitches. Each student continues to sing his pattern until all members of the class have joined. A complex rhythmic and harmonic texture results.

Improvisation carries over into rhythmic movement and solfege. For example, the teacher might play familiar holiday tunes—"We Wish You a Merry Christmas," "Happy New Year," "Happy Hanukkah"—and ask students to choose one and dance with it. The teacher, in piano improvisation, weaves the three tunes together and observes the original movements created by each of the three groups. In further improvisation in movement, class members are asked to realize one of the tunes in movement while singing another. An advanced student might sing an original melody with syllables, simultaneously playing the rhythm of the melody on a tambourine and improvising appropriate movement.

# EURYTHMICS IN SPECIAL EDUCATION

Eurhythmics has been recommended for exceptional children —for the talented because it is rich in opportunities for creative and artistic expression, and for the handicapped because it goes to the unconscious level of emotional response and provides for the education of feeling. Dalcroze himself worked with both gifted and handicapped students. In Barcelona he taught blind people. On the basis of this experience he commented that sighted children read in the facial expressions of their teachers an attitude of acceptance and approval (or the lack of it), but that blind persons miss this important non-verbal communication. In eurhythmics, interaction between teacher and class helps to compensate for the loss of usual nonverbal cues. Dalcroze suggested that blind persons approach the study of music through the relationships among space, time, and energy. He devised special exercises for developing consciousness of space and of unseen objects. The exercises were arranged according to difficulty, as were those he wrote for general use. He blindfolded some of his students who had normal eyesight and tried these exercises with them. Children as well as adults took part in this blindfold experiment. Written descriptions of twenty-one "Exercises for Developing the Sense of Space and the Muscular Sense" were provided. These were followed by twelve "Exercises for Developing Tactile Sensibility and Muscular Consciousness" and fifteen "Exercises for Developing the Auditory Faculties in their Relation to Space and the Muscular Sense." As a result of his work with blind students and his observation of similar work done by other teachers, Dalcroze began to wonder whether sighted people might learn from the blind some important facts about the use of the motor-tactile sense.

The special exercises for the blind can be read in their entirety in the eighth chapter of Dalcroze's book, *Eurhythmics, Art and Education*. Some examples follow.

Number 8, "Exercises for Developing the Sense of Space and the Muscular Sense":

Two rows of pupils facing each other. Each pupil in the first row, with outstretched arms, touches the palm of the hand of a pupil in row 2. One step backwards, then again one step forward, clapping the hand that has been released. . . . Then two steps, three steps, eight steps, twelve steps. . . . etc.

Number 9 of the same series:

Two rows, facing each other. Each pupil of row 1 going to his right along row 2, claps, keeping time, the hand of the first pupil opposite him, then the second, third, fourth, etc. The spaces between each pupil should be varied, as also the number of steps to be taken.

Number 1, "Exercises for Developing Tactile Sensibility and Muscular Consciousness":

Realize on the arms of a sighted pupil the *crescendos* and decrescendos of muscular innervation, in their relation to fullness of gesture—then execute these dynamic nuances oneself. Control is easy to establish if, in moving his arms, the pupil can place the end of his finger on different steps of a ladder or on pegs planted in the wall and serving as guide-marks.

Number 2 of the same series:

Determine the length of steps, the extent of lunges by the same method. Regulate body balance by means of the muscular sensation created by displacement of the weight of the body.

Number 1, "Exercises for Developing the Auditory Faculties in their Relation to Space and the Muscular Sense":

The pupils, standing anywhere in the room, guide themselves by the voice of the master. He moves about, uttering a sound or beating a drum from time to time; they walk in the direction of the sound. . . . The master plays the piano, the pupils, attracted by the sound, make their way towards the piano, to right or left, pass round it, retreat from it during the decrescendo, etc.

Number 8 of the same series:

Distinguish the direction of several sounds uttered simultaneously in various parts of the room.[18]

# HISTORICAL DEVELOPMENT

Essentially, Dalcroze's educational theories were stated in two books: *Rhythm, Music and Education* (1921); and *Eurhythmics, Art and Education* (1930). In these, he wrote about the reasons for the development of eurhythmics. He stressed the three areas of study and pointed out the advantages his system offered to musicians, to those interested in the other arts, and to a school. The earlier book, *Rhythm, Music and Education,* contained essays Dalcroze had written between 1898 and 1919. Probably the most important part of this collection was the 1914 statement of the sixty-six exercises Dalcroze had developed for teaching rhythmic movement, solfege, and improvisation. *Eurhythmics, Art and Education* was made up of essays written between 1922 and 1925. He included in it a chapter on "Eurhythmics and the Education of the Blind."

Three of the seven chapters in M. E. Sadler's compilation, *The Eurhythmics of Jaques-Dalcroze* (1918) were the work of Dalcroze himself. "Rhythm As a Factor in Education" was a reprinted periodical article, "Moving Plastic and Dance" had been taken from the introduction to a book, and the third was titled "Taken From the Lectures of Emile Jaques-Dalcroze." Some definite statements of his educational philosophy were made in these chapters, but the present-day reader meets two problems that obscure all of Dalcroze's writings: pre-1930 educational thought, and inadequate translation from French into English.

The *Methode Jaques-Dalcroze* [19] (1907-1914) contained suggested exercises of several kinds and music to accompany them. In the preface, Dalcroze made several statements that seem to summarize his thinking. He stated that:

—eurhythmics cannot be learned exclusively from books.

—the realization that students failed to hear in their minds the sounds represented by musical notation convinced him that intellectual study of music is inadequate.

—following the success of the eartraining exercises with adult classes, he felt sure that similar work should be done with children.

—of the three basic elements in music—melody, rhythm, and dynamics—the latter two are closely related to the physical nature of human beings and therefore a logical way to study music is through active physical response to it.

Dalcroze composed more than six hundred songs for use in eurhythmics classes. In those that he wrote for children, the words dealt with familiar childhood experiences. Among his song collections for children were *First Children's Songs and Dances, Children's Songs, New Children's Songs and Dances,* and four volumes of *Action Songs.* For older students he wrote songs, exercises in solfege, piano music, and music for violin and piano. Unlike the compositions of Kodaly and Orff, the music Dalcroze wrote for instruction has not become part of the school repertoire. His songs for children are still sung in France, but they seem inappropriate for American classrooms. Melodies were contrived and the suggested movements were stiff and mechanical, seeming strange in the con-

"Slide with Hop" from Elsa Findlay, *Rhythm and Movement: Applications of Dalcroze Eurhythmics* (Evanston, Illinois: Summy-Birchard Company, 1971), p.71. Used by permission.

text of eurhythmics. His instrumental compositions may prove more adaptable for our purposes.

In 1950, at the age of 85, Emile Jaques-Dalcroze died. His legacy to the musical world includes:

1. Three major books, plus numerous shorter discussions on movement and music theory. In addition to the original French language, translations of various articles and books are found in English, German, Italian, and Russian

2. Thirty-nine musical pageants (spectacles), including one opera

3. One hundred eight orchestral works, including transcriptions of sections of the various pageants

4. Eighty-five chamber works for many instrumental combinations

5. One hundred twenty-five piano pieces

6. Over 1,000 songs with piano accompaniment, including action songs, songs for children, folklike Swiss songs, and art songs

7. Seventy-five songs with orchestral accompaniment

8. Over 200 unaccompanied choral pieces

9. One hundred seventy-five chorus numbers with piano accompaniment

10. Two hundred chorus numbers with orchestral accompaniment

11. Three concertos for violin and orchestra

12. Two smaller works, one for violin and one for flute, both with orchestral accompaniment.[20]

Since rhythmic movement was the basic instructional procedure in the Dalcroze approach to music education, Dalcroze's ideas were taught by means of personal instruction rather than written materials. During his lifetime, the originator of eurhythmics gave his personal approval to those he felt were qualified to teach his method; as a result, the spread of eurhythmics outside the country of its origin depended on a few specially trained teachers. The first American to receive a Dalcroze certificate was Lucy Duncan Hall, who taught for many years at New York University. After the introduction of eurhythmics into the United States about 1915, Dalcroze's ideas began to influence public school music here. Those who insisted that the method be used in pure form and in its entirety found that the public schools could not provide time or space for it. Other teachers adapted some of the procedures to the needs of their classes. Still others learned specific ideas

or instructional devices and began to use them without know-
ing their source. For example, the use of walking and running
movements to represent quarter and eighth note values became
fairly widespread in the United States.

Rhythm became a catchword, the more quickly since almost no one
knew quite what it meant. Notwithstanding the usual facetious attitude of the public and the press, the classes in eurythmics grew;
teachers of music, of physical education, of dancing, and just ordinary teachers became interested; people flocked to the demonstrations
—and the usual crop of imitators soon sprang up in New York and
elsewhere.
    Eurythmics became a part of the curriculum in many private
schools where it was sometimes substituted for regular gymnastic
classes, for dancing lessons or for classwork in music.[21]

By the 1930's the method was well known among American
musicians and a few colleges and conservatories required
some work in eurhythmics. Karl Gehrkens considered the
system important enough for inclusion in his 1934 book on
instructional methods in the elementay school.

*Rhythm Training and Dalcroze Eurythmics*
The word rhythm means literally "flow" and *flow* implies movement.
Rhythm in music, therefore, always means movement, and in modern
music it implies motion in grouped units, the smaller groups being
measures and sections; the larger ones phrases, periods, and various
even longer parts.

*The Fallacy*
But in recording an approximation of this rhythmic movement in
notation it has unfortunately become necessary to use symbols standing for fixed time units, and often the instructor has fondly believed
that in teaching the learner the mathematical relations of these time
symbols he was teaching rhythm. In other words, the teacher has
shown the pupil how a whole note can be divided into two halves or
four quarters—even as is true in the case of a pie or an apple. He
explains to the pupils that $\frac{1}{2} + \frac{1}{4} + \frac{1}{4} = 1$—that is, a whole note.
He demonstrates that the dotted-eighth-sixteenth consists of two parts,
the first of which is equal to three-sixteenths, the sum of the two
therefore being four-sixteenths, which equals a quarter note.
    After such exercises in arithmetic the teacher returns to music—
and is astonished and grieved to find that his pupil cannot manage

rhythm any better than he could before. When the pupil is now confronted with the dotted-eighth-sixteenth as a problem in reading and fails to respond to it correctly the teacher calls him stupid; but it is the teacher who is stupid and it is no wonder that many intelligent modern children question the authority of their instructors and are bored by some of the dull and meaningless tasks which are still frequently imposed upon them.

But not all teachers of music are stupid, and even the stupid ones sometimes come to realize vaguely that there must be something wrong with their methods because they never seem to accomplish the ends sought. So gradually we are developing the idea of teaching rhythm as movement instead of mathematics. We are realizing that almost every child has something in him that stimulates him to respond physically to the rhythm of music heard or sung; but that this something needs to be fostered, trained, developed, organized—in short brought under control. Many of us are coming to see that the training of this rhythmic sense has a highly important educational influence upon the child's mind as well as upon his body, the result of such training being freedom, self confidence, grace, and poise— in other words a psychophysical sense of well being.

*Jacques-Dalcroze: a Reformer*
But the man who has gone farther than any one else in working this idea of physical response to rhythm into a system is Jacques-Dalcroze, and Dalcroze Eurythmics is recognized the world over as the most complete method of developing the rhythmic sense that has ever been devised.[22]

Arthur F. Becknell has made a study of the impact of Dalcroze's ideas on public school music in the United States.[23] Among the historical developments he described were the founding of the Dalcroze School of Music in New York City in 1915; emergence of the Cleveland Institute of Music as first in the United States to grant a degree in eurhythmics; and establishment of the first permanent Department of Eurhythmics at Carnegie Institute of Technology. In conference reports of the Music Supervisors National Conference and the Music Educators National Conference, he found evidence that leaders in the profession had spoken, given demonstrations, and led discussions on the Dalcroze method. Among the music educators who were most active in adapting Dalcroze principles were Karl Gehrkens, Mabelle Glenn, and Lucy Duncan

Hall. Becknell has traced the influence of Dalcroze's ideas in several of the major song series published for school use, beginning in 1936 and becoming steadily more widespread. The following quotations give further information about the early spread of the Dalcroze method.

In the United States the work is so new that it cannot yet be accurately judged by the results obtained especially as we have at present only a few qualified teachers in this country, but in Europe . . . it is taught as an obligatory subject in many of the most important conservatories and schools of Germany, Austria-Hungary, England, Russia, Switzerland, France, Belgium, and Holland, not to speak of classes in Sweden, Italy, and Spain.[24]

M. Jaques-Dalcroze will only issue a certificate authorizing a pupil to teach after he has himself tested the capacity of the would-be teacher; and since comparatively few of these authorized teachers have come to America (in 1924 there were eleven in the United States), the spread of the method here is necessarily slow.

An interesting experiment was made by one of the music supervisors in the New York public schools who had herself been a Dalcroze pupil for several years. In the *Musical Courier* for August, 1920, she summarized the ways in which she had adapted eurythmics to the teaching of music in the public schools in her district, in spite of limitations of time and actual working space.

Although there is a well-established school in Paris, the most interesting experiments there have been in connection with the theatre. . . . Of still greater importance was the introduction of a teacher of eurythmics into the training school of the Paris Opera, for it is in the presentation of lyric drama that the rhythmic principles can be most directly and satisfactorily applied.

Eurythmics has had a greater success in England, probably, than any other country save Switzerland where it originated. There is a school in London which not only provides classes for children and adults, but offers normal courses. . . . There are authorized Dalcroze teachers in the following British colonies: in Adelaide and Sydney, Australia; in New Zealand; and in Cape Town, Durban and Johannesburg, South Africa.

The most amazing phase of the progress of the method in Europe, however, is the introduction of eurythmics into the department of education in Russia. In a 1921 letter to Dalcroze, one of his pupils reported that "as the central Government bans dancing, all dancing is called 'rhythmic gymnastic.'"[25]

Since the 1963 meeting of the International Society for Music Education in Tokyo, a great deal of interest in using the Dalcroze method of instruction in Japan has been reported. At that meeting a demonstration of the method was given by Professor Yasushi Itano, who is a graduate of the Dalcroze School of Music in New York City and a member of his government's committee on education. The largest college for teacher education in Japan offers training in the Dalcroze system, and workshops are given for public school teachers throughout the country. Sometimes as many as two hundred teachers participate in one of these workshops.

Today, Hilda M. Schuster is the only authorized representative of Dalcroze in the United States, and the Dalcroze School of Music in New York City, of which she is director, is the only institution in the Americas authorized by the originator of eurhythmics to prepare teachers of the subject. In addition to a full program of teacher training classes, the Dalcroze School in New York offers a summer session lasting six weeks. An important part of the program of this particular school is its classes for children who may begin their study at the age of three. The Cleveland Institute of Music offers a bachelor's degree in eurhythmics. Chairman of the Department of Eurhythmics there is Elsa Findlay, who studied with Jaques-Dalcroze. In addition, the following institutions in various parts of the country regularly offer courses in Dalcroze eurhythmics: Hartford (Connecticut) Conservatory of Music; New England Conservatory of Music, Boston; University of Minnesota, Minneapolis; Westminster Choir College, Princeton, New Jersey; Juilliard School, New York City; Oberlin (Ohio) College; Mansfield (Pennsylvania) State Teachers College; Carnegie-Mellon Institute of Technology, Pittsburgh; University of Wisconsin, Madison; Bank Street College, New York City; New School of Social Research, New York City; Trinity College, Burlington, Vermont; Manhattan School of Music, New York City; University of Washington, Seattle; Montclair (New Jersey) State Teachers College; Peabody Conservatory, Baltimore; Kent (Ohio) State College; Hunter College, New York City; University of Southern Cali-

fornia, Los Angeles; New York University; The City College
Graduate School of Education, New York City; and University of North Carolina, Chapel Hill.

[1] Arthur F. Becknell, "A History of the Development of Dalcroze Eurhythmics
in the United States and Its Influence on the Public School Music Program."
(Doctoral Dissertation, University of Michigan, 1970), p. 13.

[2] Jack Dobbs, "Some Great Music Educators: Emile Jaques-Dalcroze," *Music
Teacher*, Vol. 47, No. 8 (August 1968), p. 14.

[3] Dobbs, p. 13.

[4] Emile Jaques-Dalcroze, "Teaching Music Through Feeling," *Etude*, Vol 39
(June 1921), p. 368.

[5] Jo Pennington, *The Importance of Being Rhythmic: A Study of the Princi-
ples of Dalcroze Eurhythmics Applied to General Education and to the Arts of
Music, Dancing, and Acting*. Based on and adapted from *Rhythm, Music and
Education* by E. Jaques-Dalcroze; with an introduction by Walter Damrosch.
New York: G. P. Putnam's Sons, 1925, pp. 26-27.

[6] Dobbs, p. 13.

[7] Emile Jaques-Dalcroze, "Eurythmics and Its Implications," trans. Frederick
Rothwell, *Musical Quarterly*, Vol. 16 (July 1930), p. 358.

[8] Emile Jaques-Dalcroze, *Eurythmics, Art and Education*. London: Chatto and
Windus, 1930, pp. 110-111.

[9] Dalcroze later discarded the term "Rhythmic Counterpoint" and substituted
"Complementary Rhythm." The new term suggests that the second rhythm pattern *completes* or complements the first.

[10] Pennington, pp. 14-26.

[11] Virginia Hoge Mead, "An Appraisal of the Dalcroze Method," report of an
article from Ohio Music Educators Association *Triad*.

[12] Dalcroze, *Eurythmics, Art and Education*, p. 107.

[13] Becknell, p. 16.

[14] Becknell, p. 16.

[15] Becknell, pp. 16-17.

[16] Becknell, p. 17.

[17] Becknell, p. 18.

[18] Dalcroze, *Eurhythmics, Art and Education*, trans. Frederick Rothwell,
pp. 145-168.

[19] *Methode Jaques-Dalcroze*.

[20] Becknell, p. 12.

[21] Pennington, p. 8.

[22] Karl W. Gehrkens, *Music in the Grade Schools* (Grades 1-6). Boston: C.
C. Birchard & Co., 1934, Chapter 10.

[23] Becknell.

[24] Grace Smith, "The Eurhythmics of Jaques-Dalcroze," *Journal of Proceedings
and Addresses of the National Education Association of the United States*. Ann
Arbor, Michigan: Published by the Association, 1915, p. 869.

[25] Pennington, p. 8.

# THE APPROACH OF ZOLTAN KODALY

The major goal of Kodaly's system of music education was to provide skills in music reading and writing to the entire population of a country. Kodaly believed that these skills were essential to the study of all aspects of the art, including its history, analysis, and performance. He believed that in Hungary everyone should receive training in the reading and writing of music just as he received training in the reading and writing of his native language, and that this musical training should come at the same time—during the early years of his formal education (see the reprinted article "Zoltan Kodaly's Legacy to Music Education" by Egon Kraus, page 123). To carry out this ideal, Kodaly instigated a program for public education in music called sol-fa teaching. It is primarily a plan for teaching choral musicianship; it stresses the skills of music reading and writing, including sightsinging and dictation; it is meant to begin as early as possible in the life of the student and to prepare him for lifelong enjoyment of music. It is based on acquisition of a vocabulary of rhythmic and melodic motives or patterns.

Like Dalcroze, Kodaly believed that fundamental knowledge of music is accessible to everyone, not just to a talented few. Both men believed that special methods of teaching could be devised that would bring basic facts and skills of

Courtesy Boosey & Hawkes, Inc., New York City.

musical communication to their students. Although Kodaly knew the work of Dalcroze and realized the importance of rhythmic movement as part of musical training, he developed a very different approach. Unlike Dalcroze, Kodaly saw his program adopted on a nationwide basis in the educational system of his own country.

Kodaly gained recognition in three separate but interrelated musical fields. His success in music education was shaped and determined by his achievements as a composer and as a musicologist. As a composer, he is best known for the orchestral suite based on his opera *Hary Janos*, for *The Peacock Variations*, and for the *Psalmus Hungaricus* for tenor solo, chorus, and orchestra. As a musicologist, he collaborated with Bela Bartok in collecting, classifying, and editing a vast number of Hungarian folk songs. For teaching school music, he developed a huge repertoire of instructional materials that included his own pedagogical compositions as well as children's choir music. He established the guidelines on which a well-defined curriculum in music education has been built.

Kodaly believed that music education should begin as early as possible in the life of the individual. Hungarian children often begin their musical study in the government's nursery schools, some at the age of two and one-half years.[1] At this age, Kodaly believed, children are most receptive; future development of both a musical ear and discriminating musical taste is enhanced if they receive the best possible instruction between the ages of three and seven. Like Orff, Kodaly believed that the individual child reenacts the musical development of his race, from primitive musical responses to a highly developed level of musicianship. The earliest lessons in music were considered the most important, whether for professional or for amateur musicians of the future, and activities and materials were organized in the same way for the beginning study. A carefully planned and systematically developed sequence of musical concepts and experiences is fundamental to the Kodaly method of instruction. Rhythmic and melodic concepts, key signatures, meter signatures, and other theoretical symbols are integrated into the study plan at carefully predetermined points. The song material in Kodaly's *Choral Method* series is arranged according to difficulty and offers concentrated practice on each level.

Kodaly shared with Orff the belief that with young children singing and movement are naturally simultaneous. In the nursery school and in the early elementary grades, singing games are an important part of the Kodaly plan. Another type of movement appropriate to this method is the traditional patterned folk dance. Early in the study of rhythm and melody, movement is used to reinforce specific ideas. When they are learning about the basic pulse of music, for example, children walk and clap in rhythm with the basic beat.

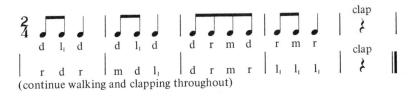

(continue walking and clapping throughout)

"No. 17" from Zoltan Kodaly, *Pentatonic Music, Volume II*, English edition by Geoffry Russell-Smith. Copyright 1958 by Zenemukiado Vallalat, Budapest. English edition copyright 1970 by Boosey & Hawkes Music Publishers Ltd., p.10. Used by permission of Boosey & Hawkes, Inc.

Many of Kodaly's *333 Elementary Exercises* may be sung in connection with basic movements such as walking, running, and marching. The second volume of his *Pentatonic Music* is subtitled "100 Little Marches." For the most part, it is considered to be the teacher's responsibility to invent appropriate rhythmic movements to accompany songs.

Kodaly expressed strong opinions on the formation of musical taste. He felt that an important goal of any music education program is the development of aesthetic sensitivity, and that such development must begin early since the individual's attitudes toward aesthetic experiences in music will be formed by the time of adolescence. An important part of the Hungarian child's education, according to Kodaly, is knowledge of his national heritage in music. This meant folk songs as well as the classics of musical literature. Kodaly planned an ordered sequence of musical materials for study at all levels, beginning with the nursery school. Some of these publications are available in the United States today:

*Pentatonic Music: Volume I—100 Hungarian Folk Songs*
*Volume II—100 Little Marches*
*333 Elementary Exercises in Sight-Singing*
*50 Nursery Songs Within the Range of 5 Notes*
*Let Us Sing Correctly: 101 Exercises in Intonation*
*Bicinia Hungarica* (Four volumes of two-part songs)
*15 Two Part Exercises*
*77 Two Part Exercises*
*66 Exercises in Two Parts*
*55 Two Part Exercises*
*44 Two Part Exercises*
*33 Two Part Exercises*
*22 Two Part Exercises*
*Tricinia Hungarica: 28 Progressive Three Part Songs*
*Epigrams: Nine Vocalises with Piano Accompaniment*
*24 Little Canons on the Black Keys*

# SOL-FA TEACHING

Reading and writing musical notation are primary goals in the Kodaly system. These skills are considered functional and prerequisite to other achievements and learnings. Just as the ability to read and write one's own language is essential to the study of various subjects in the academic curriculum, so in the Kodaly philosophy skill in music reading and writing is essential to all the various aspects of musical study. "Is it imaginable that anybody who is unable to read words can acquire a literary culture or knowledge of any kind? Equally no musical knowledge of any kind can be acquired without the reading of music." [2] Kodaly called his method sol-fa teaching, a name derived from the Tonic Sol-fa system used in England after about 1840 by John Curwen.

Actually the sol-fa system is not new nor was it Kodaly's idea. That tonic sol-fa is the medium used to carry out Kodaly's ideas is true, but this is only a basis. Kodaly wanted nothing but the best in his dream of musical literacy for every child, and so he made an intensive study of the existing systems or methods of many countries, including the French solfege system. He concluded that relative sol-fa, which he found in England, was the best medium to adapt his ideas. To this he added the use of hand signals which he also found in England, attributed to John Curwen as early as 1864. But the so-called "Kodaly method" was made by a small group of devoted followers and teachers who developed musical literacy through the use of relative sol-fa, step by step. The result today is a highly organized sequential curriculum. . . .[3]

The Curwen system was based on the principle of movable do and used syllables to represent pitches; these syllables were abbreviated by their initial letters. Rhythmic values were notated in the Curwen system by punctuation marks. Kodaly adopted the initial letters that stood for the syllable names of pitches, but he used other aids for teaching rhythmic notation. Neither Curwen nor Kodaly intended that their systems of abbreviated notation should replace the standard staff notation. Kodaly's plan is more closely related than Curwen's to standard notation, and it uses special symbols as aids in teaching pitch and duration only in the early stages of study.

l m    l s m    d' l    s m r    m r m s    m r d l,    s, s, d r    l, l, l,

"No. 50" from Zoltan Kodaly, *Pentatonic Music, Volume II*, English edition by Geoffry Russell-Smith. Copyright 1958 by Zenemukiado Vallalat, Budapest. English edition copyright 1970 by Boosey & Hawkes Music Publishers Ltd., p.21. Used by permission of Boosey & Hawkes, Inc.

Unlike Dalcroze and most other European teachers, Kodaly used the movable do system of solmization, in which syllable names indicate functions within the tonality and relationships among the constituent pitches in a given key, rather than absolute pitch. To distinguish it from the traditional European system of fixed do, Kodaly called his system Relative Sol-fa.

The essence of *relative solmisation* is that *do* can be on any line or space between the lines. To prevent it getting stuck to one spot, it should be moved about and shown in different positions. It is however the teacher's job not to overdo this. If he sees that the children are experiencing difficulty over the moving of the *do*, he must keep it in the same place for a time; during a whole lesson, or several lessons if necessary. Should however *do* become fixed rigidly to the same spot, it will be very difficult to move it to another position, even within the range of the same clef.

The ability to shift from one tonic to another is the secret of good reading. This is facilitated by using sol-fa syllables, and should be developed slowly and consistently.[4]

Relative sol-fa teaching is a well developed, sequential plan based on acquisition of a vocabulary of rhythmic and melodic motives or patterns. These patterns are analogous to the words and phrases that make up initial learning experiences in language. The child encounters rhythmic and melodic motives first through singing and hearing them. They are abstracted from the musical context and repeated many times. The child comes to recognize them first as sounds, then in other forms of concrete and spatial representation. These representations might include colored sticks or children standing alone and with linked arms ( | | ⊓ | ) to express rhythmic motives; big body motion describing the melody line, later transcribed to hand signals and eventually reduced to staff notation. Only after a child is thoroughly familiar with rhythmic and melodic patterns through a variety of experiences is the transference to staff notation consciously learned (see the reprinted article "Kodaly and Education: A Musicological Note" by Alexander L. Ringer, page 145). In this way the earliest experiences with notation, like the reading of language, represent ideas the child is already using. The repertoire of musical patterns is used in establishing interrelationships among the constituent tones of a key, in elementary sightsinging and in creative ways. These syllable names and abbreviations are used in the Kodaly system:

do  re  mi  fa  so[5]  la  ti  do
d   r   m   f   s   l   t   d'

After the syllable ti in the ascending order of the scale tones,

Model School, Needham, Massachusetts. Courtesy Kodaly Musical Training Institute.

the next or eighth tone in the series (do) is marked with an apostrophe. When tones above this high do are used, they are similarly marked. Tones below the key tone in a descending order, ti, la, and sol, for example, are identified by commas: sol, la, ti, do re mi fa sol la ti do' re' mi'. Early in their musical study children use these syllables in singing at different pitch levels, so that the idea of movable do becomes a practical reality to them.

Syllable names and functions of pitches are introduced in

a definite order that is strictly followed. Beginning with the so-called universal chant of childhood, the descending minor third or sol-mi, pitches are introduced one at a time.

sol mi
la  sol mi
la  sol mi do
la  sol mi re do
fa
ti [6]

There is much reinforcement of the scale tones, even when so few are involved: Kodaly wrote dozens of exercises restricted to a range of two, three, four, or five tones. In the following exercise, do is on G.

"No. 29" from Zoltan Kodaly, *333 Elementary Exercises*. Copyright 1941 by Zoltan Kodaly, renewed 1969. English edition copyright 1963 by Boosey & Co. Ltd., p.3. Used by permission of Boosey & Hawkes, Inc.

In contrast with systems that introduce all eight tones of the major scale as early as possible, this system adds la and sol below the tonal center to the repertoire of pitches before completing the major scale within an octave.

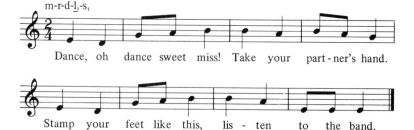

"No. 47" from Zoltan Kodaly, *Fifty Nursery Songs*, English edition by Percy M. Young. Copyright 1962 by Zoltan Kodaly. Revised English edition copyright 1970 by Boosey & Hawkes Music Publishers Ltd., p.47. Used by permission of Boosey & Hawkes, Inc.

When students have acquired full use of the diatonic range and the chromatic syllables fi, si, and ta, they may also use the sol-fa syllables to learn the principles of modulation.

"No. 3" from Zoltan Kodaly, *Tricinia*, English edition by Percy M. Young. Copyright 1954 by Zenemukiado Vallalat, Budapest. English edition copyright 1964 by Boosey & Hawkes Music Publishers Ltd., p.9. Used by permission of Boosey & Hawkes, Inc.

Many examples of songs built on the limited number of pitches used at this stage are found in Hungarian folk music. However, it was because Kodaly could not find enough songs with small range and simple rhythms that he wrote his *Fifty Nursery Songs*. He often expressed surprise that other countries wished to adapt his method, and his first advice to teachers in foreign countries was to identify a large body of folk material of their own country.

Kodaly considered fa and ti hardest of the diatonic scale degrees to sing in tune, particularly for children.

Kodaly's music for young children is based initially on the pentatonic, the five-note scale which omits the fourth and seventh. There are two basic reasons for this. Firstly, children (and incidentally, primitive peoples as well) will tend to sing the fourth slightly sharp and the seventh slightly flat. So by removing these notes—*fa* and *ti*—from the scale and having only *do-re-me-so-la*, this difficulty is immediately overcome. Secondly, the pitch distance between the fourth and the seventh is an awkward "unsingable" interval which is almost impossible for anyone except experienced singers to get in tune.[7]

Fa and ti were introduced in Kodaly's *Bicinia Hungarica* Volume I, and he suggested that in readiness for reading them, special two-part exercises in intonation be sung. These exercises stress the relationship of fa and ti with neighboring scale tones.

The basic mode of instruction in Kodaly's method is singing. He believed that the voice is the most immediate and personal way of expressing oneself in music, and he realized that in many Hungarian schools instruments of various kinds would be unavailable. By means of vocal music the ear could best be trained to distinguish intervals and to keep the young musician in tune. As in the Dalcroze method, such training as this preceded instrumental study. It was expected to enhance the enjoyment of music of adults in choral groups and attending concerts. One of the basic ideas underlying the Kodaly method is that singing should be done in an especially careful way—that students should be taught to use their voices as well as possible. Pure tone and accurate intonation are required. Development of inner hearing contributes to this ideal, as does the fact that children gain a great deal of experience in singing.

Kodaly believed that voices are best accompanied by other voices rather than by instruments. In this way the singer learns the skills of choral singing, such as blending his voice with other voices, maintaining his part independently of other singers, and most important in Kodaly's opinion, singing in tune. Children imitate the teacher's example in learning about melody and phrasing. The teacher also sings musical examples in which children listen for various other musical elements. Correct intonation is developed through exercises, like the ones in *Let Us Sing Correctly* where all tones are of long duration, so that singers may tune their voices with others. In the earliest exercises one part moves while the other remains constant. These exercises are meant to be sung initially from hand signs given by the teacher; later the same exercises may be read from the book. Part singing is first introduced through easy canons and melodic ostinatos. The collection

"No. 35" from Zoltan Kodaly, *66 Two-Part Exercises,* English edition by Percy M. Young. Copyright 1963 by Zenemukiado Vallalat, Budapest. English edition copyright 1964 by Boosey & Hawkes Music Publishers Ltd., p.23. Used by permission of Boosey & Hawkes, Inc.

*Let Us Sing Correctly* was designed for developing clear intonation. One of the ways to achieve independence in part singing is through exercises using canonic imitation, as in *Sixty-Six Two-Part Exercises* and *Fifteen Two-Part Exercises.* Skill in sightsinging is developed progressively through Kodaly's *Seventy-Seven, Sixty-Six, Fifty-Five, Forty-Four, Thirty-Three,* and *Twenty-Two Two-Part Exercises,* the last being the most difficult and not really intended for children's classes. One hundred eight selections for two-part singing are contained in the four volumes of *Bicinia Hungarica.* While

"No. 3" from Zoltan Kodaly, *Bicinia Hungarica, Volume I,* English edition by Percy M. Young. Copyright 1941 by Zoltan Kodaly, renewed 1969. Revised English edition copyright 1968 by Boosey & Co. Ltd., p.9. Used by permission of Boosey & Hawkes, Inc.

Model School, Needham, Massachusetts. Courtesy Kodaly Musical Training Institute.

their musical and pedagogical value is unquestionable, their use outside the country of their origin will be limited because of the essentially Hungarian character of the melodies. There is undoubtedly a need for a similar American collection of two-part folk songs, according to Kodaly followers.

Among the techniques for strengthening part singing and inner hearing are several in which singers exchange parts at a signal from the teacher. This practice is begun in the elementary school years.

Through a process called automatic recognition, children build a vocabulary of rhythmic and melodic patterns.

We isolate and teach units (rhythmic and melodic "microstructures"), and after constant repetition in new circumstances the child discovers for himself the relations of the sounds in time (rhythm) and in pitch (interval).

The intervals are connected with hand-signals and sol-fa syllables on the basis of a movable *do,* and the rhythmic relations are connected with special names (ta, ti-ti, etc.).[8]

These musical microstructures are sung, written, practiced in hand signs, represented in movement, and used in improvisation. Like a word or phrase he has used many times in language, a specific musical motive is recognized by the child, first in isolation and then in a musical context. Children may observe similarities and dissimilarities among motives, find familiar patterns in new songs, and analyze the starting motives of songs and group together all the songs that begin with the same melodic pattern.

*Automatically-recognized motives of music become part of the "activity repertoire" of the child;* he recalls, recognizes, sings, sounds, makes hand signals. Motives appear in new situations all the time and are fixed in their so-fa and rhythmical form.

If the child has good ability to read from notes he will do it not through outer direction but by a sort of inner compulsion on the basis of his former knowledge. . . . *The child owns a rich inner repertoire of motives and he chooses from them* when writing down a new rhythm or melody, or when reading aloud an unknown song.[9]

There is a great deal of practice on the children's vocabulary of melodic patterns. The melodic interval sol mi (5-3), for example, is isolated and recognized in as many familiar songs as possible. Children sing questions and answers on the two tones:

Where is El-len?    Here I am.
s    s m m    s    s m

Pictorial representations are used, both with and without the musical staff, in discussing which tone is higher and which lower. Body movements and hand signs reinforce the pitch relationship.

One of the distinguishing characteristics of the Kodaly

"Hand Signal Chart" from Arpad Darazs and Stephen Jay, *Sight and Sound, Teachers Manual* (New York: Boosey & Hawkes, Inc., 1965), p.14. Used by permission.

*Hand Signal Chart*

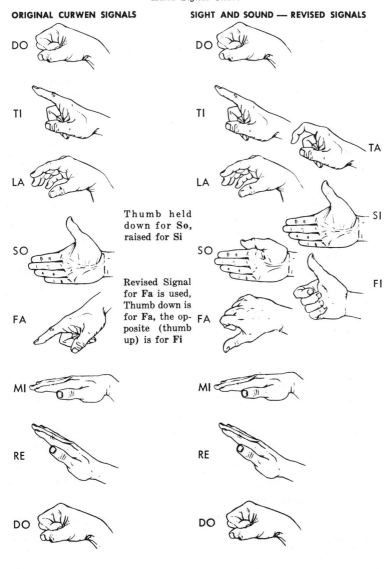

system is the use of hand signs to represent melodic inter-relationships. In the nineteenth century, hand signs were associated with the Tonic Sol-fa method of John Curwen. They utilize the pull of certain scale tones toward the tonal center and toward the fairly stationary sounds of mi and sol: ti, represented by pointing upward, tends toward do; fa, with the thumb pointing downward, tends toward mi; re, with the hand pointing obliquely upward, also tends toward mi. Like the sol-fa syllables themselves, the idea that each tone of the scale expresses a feeling of relative stability or instability in relation to the other scale tones is an old idea. In the nine-teenth century it was called the mental effects of tones, and was found in some American music textbooks of that period. Hand signs are used to teach interval relationships. Like the sounds they represent, they are introduced in a strict order, beginning with sol-mi and continuing with one syllable at a time. Small children often make these signs with both hands simultaneously. An outstanding teacher of the Kodaly method stated that the real purpose of hand signs is to put a melody into space.[10]

The child's experiences reinforce each other and eventually lead to automatic recognition of rhythmic, as well as melodic, sounds and symbols. In the study of quarter rests, for exam-ple, the student, as he listens to a song or exercise, discovers a silence in the music that has the duration of a quarter note. As he sings in imitation of the teacher, he produces the same silence within the music. He claps the rhythm of the song or exercise he is singing, and observes the rest with appropriate silence. Later there will be other games involving clapping or tapping that will reinforce the concept he is formulating. Pic-torial representations are used in textbooks in Hungary to show durations of tones as well as rests. The size and the grouping of pictures can be used to illustrate rhythmic ideas found in certain songs.

Rhythm patterns, like melody patterns, are introduced ac-cording to a carefully ordered sequence of difficulty, through the medium of folk song material. Once basic pulse is well established, quarter-note values are learned through the experience of singing and hearing them, isolating them in songs, and representing them by means of the time name ta and by line notation of the standard quarter note or a stem without note head. Eighth notes written in pairs as two stems joined by a ligature are introduced and practiced next, followed by combinations of quarters and eighths. These rhythm patterns are reinforced in several ways, especially in pictorial representation, respondent games, and body movement. Half notes are represented by the time name ta-a, dotted half notes by ta-a-a, and whole notes by ta-a-a-a. In the process of teaching children to read music, special written symbols represent duration as well as pitch. In materials prepared for American classes, stems and flags alone, without note heads, are used to represent the quarter-note and eighth-note values when first introduced. In the materials Kodaly prepared, standard notes and rests are used, but often without the staff. Today, Hungarian teachers use rhythmic stems without noteheads in the classroom before teaching conventional rhythmic notation. Hungarian elementary school textbooks sometimes use stems and flags alone.

Initially one should devise some simple pictorial representation of the rhythm elements which correspond with the single down stroke of the crotchet (quarter-note) and the two down strokes joined by a ligature for the pair of quavers (eighth notes). A good example, taken from an early text book by Kodaly and Professor Adam, is to use pictures of boots: large boots for the slower steps of father, and pairs of small boots to represent the faster steps of the child who takes two steps to every one stride of his father. Once this idea has become established in the child's mind, pictorial representation can give way to conventional rhythm symbols.[11]

Helga Szabo, an authority on the Kodaly method, presented an interesting way of teaching children to recall rhythm patterns. From Kodaly's *Pentatonic Music* Volume III, children sang exercises in sol-fa; other children responded by clapping the rhythms of these exercises from memory.[12] Children acquire their first practice in writing melodic notation by placing note heads on a large staff. In preparation for writing rhythms, they use sticks to represent Kodaly's staffless rhythmic notation.

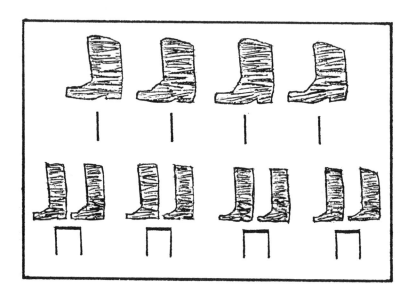

From Helga Szabo, *The Kodaly Concept of Music Education*, English edition by Geoffry Russell-Smith (London: Boosey & Hawkes Music Publishers Ltd., 1969), p.9. Used by permission of Boosey & Hawkes, Inc.

The expanding vocabulary of patterns in rhythm and melody is used as a basis for several learning procedures other than reading and writing notation. Creative activities in the Kodaly system are centered around the patterns or motives children know. Games, songs, and exercises are improvised with these musical microstructures as material. Definite plans and goals are kept in mind during improvisation; aimless exploration of sounds is discouraged. Children analyze the music that other members of their class have improvised.

Some type of improvisation can be linked up with every stage of the teaching material with singing classes. But it should never be forgot-

ten that improvisation is a game and has its value so long as it stimulates. Improvisation depends on knowledge. The student who understands the musical material truly and deeply and has acquired the
necessary skill will improvise easily.[13]

In the instructional system Kodaly established, listening
was one of the skills contributing to general musicianship. It
was related to the primary goals of the method: correct singing and skill in reading and writing notation. Often listening
selections were short and were chosen to illustrate some particular musical concept. For example, children studying a
particular melodic pattern would be asked to listen for it in a
recorded excerpt. In some of the materials Kodaly wrote for
the Hungarian schools, brief excerpts from musical scores
were provided for children to observe while listening to the
examples on recordings. The basic vocabulary of rhythmic
and melodic motives is also used in the study of musical
form. By combining or expanding familiar patterns, students
can build phrases and periods. They improvise question-
answer phrases. In addition, they analyze the melodies in
Kodaly's *333 Elementary Exercises* by labeling the phrases
with letters such as ABA.

Many ear training exercises are directed toward development of a skill called inner hearing. Children learn to
recognize intervals, to distinguish interrelationships among
scale tones, and to sing whole songs or exercises silently.
These exercises begin in kindergarten, when children inter-
rupt their singing at a signal from the teacher to sing
silently until the next signal indicates that they are to sing
aloud again. Silent singing is used also when children begin
learning to sing in parts. To develop inner hearing, children
may read a short song or exercise silently from the blackboard. After they have memorized it, the music is erased
and they sing it aloud.

Kodaly recommended that the first instrument children
use should be a xylophone with removable bars. Beginning
with two bars for playing sol-mi, the teacher and class add
other bars as the corresponding scale degrees are introduced.

The recorder is recommended as the second instrument to which children are introduced. In playing it they learn the letter names of absolute pitches and corresponding names of lines and spaces on the treble staff. The study of piano is deferred until students have a good background in vocal music, and ideally can prehear musical notation as it is read. Kodaly recommended that the study of piano begin with the black keys, and that two-part canons be used to develop independence between the hands. He suggested that two-part canons best illustrate the principle of polyphony when the pianist plays both parts by reading from a single line of notation.[14]

"No. 1" from Zoltan Kodaly, *Twenty Four Little Canons on the Black Keys.* Copyright 1954 by Zenemukiado Vallalat, Budapest. Copyright assigned 1957 to Boosey & Co. Ltd., p.4. Used by permission of Boosey & Hawkes, Inc.

# THE INSTRUCTIONAL REPERTOIRE

Kodaly believed that only the best musical literature should be used in the instructional repertoire. Children, he thought, are particularly sensitive to works of art, and should experience only serious compositions of a high quality. In order to provide such works in the smaller forms needed as teaching material, contemporary composers should write music for children. Kodaly maintained, however, that not every gifted composer is suited to writing music for children and stated that the main prerequisite for such a composer is to have the soul and spirit of a child. Songs contrived according to an adult's concept of childhood tastes and understandings should be eliminated. Commercial popular songs and even songs from operettas and Broadway shows are considered of doubtful pedagogical value in the Kodaly philosophy. He considered that music of an inferior quality actually is harmful to the development of musical taste, and that dwelling on such music in childhood would handicap later appreciation and enjoyment of better music. Attitudes and behaviors shaped in the early years, he thought, were influenced by music used in teaching. Teaching a low quality of instructional materials would result in a poorer quality of musical experiences, not only during a vital period of concept formation, but in later life as well. "Kodaly's premise is that the small child learns first through singing games, next through the folk songs of his own region and country, then through international folk song which is a bridge to art form and the classics of composed music." [15] Singing games are used in nursery and kindergarten classes because they are a natural activity of childhood, combining movement with music. They are a part of the child's cultural heritage, traditional songs with patterned movements that are inseparable from the songs themselves.

Two stages are specified in the learning of folk songs. First the student learns a considerable number of folk song of his own country, even of his own region, then his repertoire is extended to include the folk music of other peoples (see the reprinted article "Folk Song in Pedagogy" by Zoltan Kodaly, page 141). Folk music has been called a natural subject matter for teaching. Several reasons for this are given by the Hungarian teachers who are implementing the Kodaly method and by their American counterparts teaching what they call the authentic Kodaly concept in this country. Folk music can be considered part of the culture indigenous to a particular people, expressing shared thoughts and feelings that symbolize a kind of unity within the nation and with the past. The folk songs of their own country are, in the words of several outstanding Hungarian teachers, a "musical mother tongue" for Hungarian children, and according to Kodaly, for children of every culture.

Farmer Jacob

Folk-song

*Sol-fa* indications have been omitted from this piece to provide an opportunity for the young singers to find the 'doh' for themselves.

This music is considered closest to the life experiences of rural children and to the cultural heritage of urban ones. Folk music is a virtually limitless source of the musical motives and patterns that are essential in the Kodaly plan. One Hungarian teacher has called it "the inexhaustible storehouse of simple forms, rhythms, and melodies, which has gained its richness of today through long and multiple usage, and which is most suitable to serve as a means of approaching the classics." [16] Many folk songs are in the pentatonic mode and Kodaly, like Orff, considered this mode easiest and most natural for children to learn in their early lessons. There is a close relationship in the songs between music and language.

The singing of folksongs must form a part of every music lesson; not only to provide practice in them for their own sake, but to maintain continuity and also to awaken, develop and maintain the sense of relationship between music and the language. For there is no denying that it is here, in folksong, that the most perfect relationship between music and language can be found. [17]

Folk songs of other lands are added next to the student's repertoire.

Kodaly had definite purposes in mind when he compiled the various books in his instructional series. The four volumes of *Pentatonic Music* supplemented available folk song material; however only the first two volumes have been published in the United States. Volume One of *Pentatonic Music* contains one hundred Hungarian folk songs notated in sol-fa initials and notes without a staff. Volume Two is used at the kindergarten level to establish the feeling for pulse through marching, walking, or clapping the beat. Melodies in this volume are considered simple enough for the youngest school child. To implement his idea that scale tones should be introduced gradually and practiced a great deal, Kodaly grouped together nineteen studies using the two tones do and re at the beginning of the *333 Elementary Exercises*. The next thirty-six exercises are built on three tones: eleven exercises on do-la-so, seventeen on re-do-la, and eight on mi-re-do.

Some of the materials Kodaly wrote were intended to be used in a cyclical way. The *50 Nursery Songs*, for example, are learned in kindergarten by rote. Children in the primary grades read the same songs from the book. A few of these songs are reprinted in *333 Elementary Exercises* for the same purpose.

# HISTORICAL DEVELOPMENT

The Kodaly method of music education originated under conditions that were favorable to the goal of teaching all children to read and write music. In state-controlled schools with a long heritage of strict academic training in the European style, it was possible to establish in Hungary a structured curriculum for vocal music classes on a nationwide scale. In Socialist Hungary, goals for music education are established by the State. Instructional materials are specified, and standards of achievement have been defined for each grade level, from the nursery school through the institutions that train teachers. For most children, classes in vocal music meeting twice a week for forty-five minutes are a requirement through the eighth grade. In the last two years of public school, choral training is emphasized. Instrumental study is not encouraged until children can read and write music at a certain level, and is not generally considered a part of the course offerings for everyone. Teachers of this method feel that "until children can pre-hear the note they are going to produce, they cannot produce that note in tune except on a keyboard." [18]

Instrumental music teaching has its own organization and school system in Hungary. These are called Music Schools, as opposed to the music primary schools where music is taught every day and is a regular part of the curriculum. The Music Schools are a different organization. They meet after school hours and there is a program 6 years long which includes private instrumental music lessons and simultaneous solfege classes.[19]

In addition, there are Music Primary Schools in which the study of vocal music is more intensive than in the other primary and elementary schools. Children are selected on the basis of musical tests. About 130 Music Primary Schools have been established since 1950.

In 1950, Mrs. Marta Nemesszeghy established, with Kodaly's help and encouragement, the first so-called Singing Primary School in

Kecskemet, Kodaly's birthplace, an agricultural town of 60,000 of largely peasant population. This type of school was no different from any other school in Hungary except that it had music every day in the week, as opposed to the more normal twice a week. This school was developed year by year with a new music curriculum worked out by Mrs. Nemesszeghy, the school's visionary director.[20]

Instructional principles and procedures that were developed for a country roughly the size of Indiana have spread in recent years to many countries. At the 1958 conference of the International Society for Music Education, Jeno Adam introduced the Kodaly method. At successive meetings of the conference in 1961 and 1963 other Hungarian specialists lectured on it, and in 1964 Kodaly addressed the conference, which that year was held in Budapest. Teachers from several nations have visited Hungary and many of them spoke with Kodaly in person. In these ways the ideas basic to his method have been carried to the Soviet Union, Czechoslovakia, Denmark, Finland, France, West Germany, Belgium, Argentina, Chile, Peru, Switzerland, Canada, Japan, and Australia. Like the ideas of Dalcroze and Orff, the principles of the Kodaly method were brought to the United States by Europeans now living in this country and by Americans who went to Europe to study. Arpad Darazs, Katinka Daniel, Tibor Bachmann, and Laszlo Halasz made American adaptations of the method from which publications have already resulted or will result. Jeno Adam worked closely with Kodaly, and it was Adam who first presented the method in writing. The original pedagogical sequence was a result of Adam's work. His manual for Hungarian teachers has been translated into English by Louis Boros and others. Volume One, for grades one through four, is titled *Growing in Music with Movable Do*. The Boros translation contains a detailed, explicit plan for teaching music reading, the writing of rhythmic and melodic notation, and ear training. There are 113 songs adapted from Hungarian folklore. The instructional plan uses sol-fa syllables and their initial letters, stem notation to indicate rhythmic values, hand signs, rhythm names such as ta and ti-ti, and a symbol called the movable do clef that indicates the position of do on the staff.

Mary Helen Richards published a series of song books and charts with American songs and based on the principle of pictorial representation of rhythmic and melodic patterns. Denise Bacon organized summer courses at the Dana School of Music in Wellesley, Massachusetts, and presented some of the leading Hungarian music educators as teachers and lecturers. Following her year of study in Hungary (1967-68) and a year of experimental teaching in the Winchester, Massachusetts, public schools, the Kodaly Musical Training Institute opened in September 1969 with Miss Bacon as director. Its program, developed with the help and support of Mrs. Zoltan Kodaly, Martha Nemesszeghy, and the Hungarian Minister of Education, includes certificate, diploma, and summer courses both here and in Hungary.

Possibly most important of the problems of adopting or adapting the Kodaly method for American public schools is the question of materials. The study of folk songs was vital to Kodaly's plan for music education. In each of the countries that has adopted Kodaly's principles, efforts have been made to gather and classify the folk music of that country for use in place of the Hungarian songs. Kodaly believed that every nationality has a wealth of folk music that can be used to teach basic elements of musical structure, and he stated that the United States has the richest possibility of all, because of its diversified ethnic groups. "The life of folk music changes from country to country and from time to time. Other nations cannot follow the peculiar road of Hungarian development." [21] He suggested that the 40,000 folk songs in the Library of Congress Archive of American Folk Song be used as a major resource. For many years, the compilers of textbooks for public school music in the United States have included folk songs from various parts of the country, with appropriate recognition for the heritage of various groups—the Scottish in North Carolina, Scandinavians in Minnesota, and so on. One American teacher of the Kodaly method has advised:

I believe that we cannot imitate exactly the Hungarian methods. We cannot use their song material, we cannot thoughtlessly or carelessly adopt their curriculum or all of their teaching techniques. However, the conception, the aims, the goals, remain international, as binding as the unity in all humanity which Kodaly spoke about when he was in America.[22]

[1] Katalin Forrai, "Zoltan Kodaly's Reflections on Music Education," a lecture delivered at the Dana School of Music Summer Teacher Training Workshop, 1969, p. 3.

[2] Zoltan Kodaly, *Visszatekintes* (published by Zenemukiado, 1964). Quoted in Helga Szabo, *The Kodaly Concept of Music Education*. English edition by Geoffry Russell-Smith (London: Boosey and Hawkes, Ltd., 1969), p. 10.

[3] Denise Bacon, "The Kodaly Method in Relation to Total Education," published in the December 1968 issue of *Independent School Bulletin* as "Can We Afford to Ignore the Kodaly Method?"

[4] Kodaly, *Visszatekintes*, p. 13.

[5] Sol is normally used in the United States, but Hungarian children sing so. So may be easier than sol, especially when followed by the syllable la.

[6] Helga Szabo, *The Kodaly Concept of Music Education*. English edition by Geoffry Russell-Smith (London: Boosey and Hawkes, 1969).

[7] Geoffry Russell-Smith, "Introducing Kodaly Principles into Elementary Teaching," *Music Educators Journal*, Vol. 54 (November 1967), p. 43.

[8] Klara Kokas, "Kodaly's Concept in Children's Education," *Music Journal*, Vol. 29, No. 7 (September 1971), p. 50.

[9] Klara Kokas, "The Transfer Effect of the Kodaly Method of Music Education," a lecture delivered at the Teacher Training Workshop, Dana School of Music, Wellesley, Massachusetts, August 8, 1969.

[10] Klara Kokas, "The Transfer Effect of the Kodaly Method of Music Education," p. 5.

[11] Szabo, p. 9.

[12] Szabo, record album.

[13] Helga Szabo, "The Use of Improvisation in Children's Musical Development," a lecture given at the Kodaly Musical Training Institute, Inc., summer course at the University of Bridgeport (Connecticut), July 24, 1971.

[14] Szabo, p. 20.

[15] Denise Bacon, "Can the Kodaly Method Be Successfully Adapted Here?" *Musart*, Vol 22 (April-May 1970), p. 14.

[16] Laszlo Vikar, "Folk Music and Music Education," a lecture given at the Dana School of Music Teacher Training Workshop, Wellesley, Massachusetts, August 18-19, 1969.

[17] Kodaly, *Visszatekintes*, p. 13.

[18] Geoffry Russell-Smith, "Introducing Kodaly Principles into Elementary Teaching," *Music Educators Journal*, Vol. 54 (November 1967), p. 44.

[19] Elizabeth McLaughlin, "The Significance of the Kodaly Conception in America," a lecture given at the Summer Teacher Training Workshop, Dana School of Music, Wellesley, Massachusetts, August 2, 1969.

[20] Bacon, "Can the Kodaly Method Be Successfully Adapted Here?" p. 14.

[21] Vikar.

[22] McLaughlin.

# THE APPROACH OF CARL ORFF

her zlich

The central idea on which Carl Orff based his approach to music education is that music, movement, and speech are inseparable, and that they form a unity Orff called elemental music. He had observed that when children express themselves in natural and unstructured situations, they use music, movement, and speech together, rather than separately. A child who is dancing often sings or chants; when a child sings, he often moves in rhythm with his singing. Orff used the word elemental to mean primal and rudimentary, and to refer to personal expression made naturally through music. In developing his instructional approach, Orff reached back to the early stages of cultural development, when music was an untrained, unsophisticated mode of expression, inseparable from movement and speech and always involved active participation.

Orff accepted the theory that the historical development of music is reenacted in the life of each individual. The child is considered a primitive being, whose early musical responses are like those ethnomusicologists see in the peoples of underdeveloped countries. On the basis of this assumption, Orff determined that music education should begin with the simplest concepts and the simplest songs. A gradual, cumulative sequence of learning experiences resulted from this assumption. The theory that each child re-lives the course of musical development finds little agree-ment among educators today, but the related plan of struc-turing learning material in a progression of small increments from the simplest to the most complex finds widespread ac-ceptance. Ideally, Orff's *Schulwerk* should begin in early childhood, and should make use of the child's own musical experiences as material for the instructional process. The child's own name, familiar words, sayings and quotations are used in rhythmic chanting and in singing. The child hears his name spoken rhythmically, then sings it, and later reads and writes its rhythm in notation. Melodic intervals are learned, as are rhythm patterns, through singing them, say-ing them, moving to them, and playing them. Instruments are used from the earliest sessions in the course. By taking a simple motive, repeating it, and building on it, the child is able to succeed. He is using simple materials with which he can work, and he is able to develop them into something satisfying.

Orff found in the Eurhythmics of Jaques-Dalcroze more than one principle he was able to share. Most important of these in its effect on Orff's work was the idea that rhythm is strongest of the elements of music; that the most primitive and most natural musical responses of the human personality are rhythmic in nature; and that the logical starting point for education in music is rhythm. Through his concept of elemental music, Orff planned to make this idea work. Since rhythm is the shared element in speech, movement, and music, it is the logical starting point in *Schulwerk*. The belief that rhythm is the vital element in music led directly to the development of a special ensemble of instruments. In Orff's philosophy, as in that of Dalcroze, the study of piano, violin, and other standard instruments should be preceded by the development of certain musical skills: hearing, recog-nizing and singing prescribed melodic intervals, and recog-nizing and playing prescribed rhythms.

In the Orff method, creativity is most important. His in-structional plan includes provisions for several kinds of original work on a continuing basis. Children explore the sounds of words, melodies, and instruments. They choose or invent rhythmic and melodic fragments and use them to create accompaniment figures, introductions and codas, perhaps a whole song. The early instructional activities are like musical games, and indeed often are built upon children's traditional games. The teacher should be prepared to help children notate their musical ideas, evaluate the music they produce, and relate their creative efforts to the study of musical form and style. Orff's description of his educational plan included the suggestion that teachers who are themselves creative, flexible, and open to new ideas are best suited to fostering these characteristics, inherent in the method itself, in their students.

Most methodical, dogmatic people derive scant pleasure from it, but those who are artistic and who are improvisers by temperament enjoy it all the more. Every phase of *Schulwerk* will always provide stimulation for new independent growth; therefore it is never conclusive and settled, but always developing, always growing, always flowing. Herein of course lies a great danger, that of development in the wrong direction. Further independent growth presupposes basic specialist training and absolute familiarity with the style, the possibilities and the aims of *Schulwerk*.[1]

Elemental music is intensely personal, based on communicative performance. Its materials are ideally the musical ideas of the children themselves, with the *Schulwerk* compositions as models and a carefully planned melodic and rhythmic vocabulary as a framework. It is primitive, childlike, natural, physical—drawing on the activities of the child at play for beginnings and points of reference in the teaching process. The concept of elemental music includes the assumption that a child relives, through his learning experiences, the musical development of mankind. His earliest musical experiences, then, are primordial: calls, crys, chants, stamping, bending, and whirling. In elemental music, speaking, singing, and moving are not separate acts, but like the most natural, genuine musical expression, they become a composite.

The instructional materials Orff prepared for publication

were intended to preserve his ideas and to transmit them to his students and other followers. They were written during the process of carrying out a series of broadcasts with children, and after some years of teaching in which his philosophy had been formulated and his procedures shaped. As in the Dalcroze method, creativity in the form of improvisation was a major goal of the program. Also like Dalcroze, Orff had definite ideas about how improvisation would be carried out. He stated often and emphatically that the songs he wrote for children's classes were intended only as models. Several characteristics that were inherent in Orff's philosophy of music and education were clearly evident in his instructional materials: (1) Pentatonic mode was used throughout the entire first volume of the *Schulwerk*. (2) Ostinato patterns and borduns, which he expected children to create in their classroom, were consistently written in the model pieces he provided. (3) Like Kodaly, Orff chose music for instructional use that had a strong nationalistic flavor in the sense that it was related to the folksongs and other music that was a familiar part of the childhood experiences of a particular part of the world. (Nevertheless Orff is a universalist, and his injunctions to teachers all over the world indicate that he wishes them to use the music of their own heritage and idiom.) (4) Motives were taken from the song and used in the introduction and accompaniment of the song. (5) The distinctive Orff ensemble of instruments was used. (6) A basic part of the idea of elemental music is seen in the published volumes of *Schulwerk:* the chants and calls of childhood, especially the so-called universal chant of childhood, the descending minor third, are used in the beginning. It is apparent that Orff has sought the early, simple experiences in the child's musical life as a beginning point for formal instruction. His intention to arrange the learning experiences that follow in a gradual progression from simple to difficult is apparent in the written materials. (7) Speech patterns, beginning with single words and progressing to more complex activities such as speech canons, are presented in the published *Schulwerk*.

"The Day Is Now Over" from *Music for Children* illus-

The day is now over

Orff. D. H. translation

sends down His an - gels to watch o'er their fate.

"No. 18, The Day Is Now Over" from Carl Orff and Gunild Keetman, *Music for Children, Volume I: Pentatonic*, English adaptation by Doreen Hall and Arnold Walter (Mainz: B. Schott's Sohne, 1960), p.19. Used by permission of Belwin-Mills Publishing Corp.

trates important characteristics of the Orff instructional repertoire.

—Ostinato patterns are used extensively and help to develop independence and interdependence of voices (parts). The combination of several ostinatos is a frequently used device which involves several players in addition to the singers, and encourages ensemble playing.

—Like most of the songs Orff published for instructional use, this one appears in a complete and symmetrical setting with introduction and accompaniment. (Many of the songs also have codas.)

—Orff has used the simplest of motives, extracted from the melody itself, to create the introduction and the accompaniment, the same way he intends that students create their own settings.

—The pentatonic mode can be used in a texture made of several lines (six in this case) without substantial dissonances.

—The mood, a delicate quality that pervades Orff's instructional repertoire is evident in the orchestration and in the words.

—The "orchestration" is typical of *Schulwerk*.

# SPEECH

Speech as a part of the musical experience is a distinguishing characteristic of the Orff-Schulwerk approach. Orff made this a part of his plan because he felt that a gradual progression from speech patterns to rhythmic activities, and then to song, is most natural for the child. The planned sequence begins with speech, continues with body rhythms such as clapping or tapping, and culminates in playing instruments. Orff facilitated the process by turning nursery rhymes, calls, chants, and traditional sayings into musical experiences. Each teacher is to make use of the nursery rhymes, sayings, and children's names that are already familiar to his class. Children create music based on the rhythm patterns of these and other words. For example, sometimes teachers list the first names of some of the children, and the class organizes these in an order that produces interesting rhythms. Then the list may be set to music. Or, short phrases may be built from the rhythm patterns of some of the names.[2]

Jon - a - thon   Jon - a - thon   Nan - cy   Jill

From Ruth Pollock Hamm, "The Challenge of the Orff Approach for Elementary Music Education," *Musart*, Vol. 22 (April-May 1970), p.16. Used by permission.

Concepts such as meter, accent, and anacrusis are introduced in speech patterns, reinforced in other activities, then studied in a musical context. For example, the concept of canon is very effectively introduced through speech. Groups of children chant a phrase or sentence that is made up of interesting, varied rhythms. Using the idea of a round, one group begins and, at a point where rhythmic contrast has been noticed, the second group begins. The third group begins when the second has reached the predetermined point. Children caught up in the creative process will produce an endless variety of words, phrases, household sayings, and rhymes that can be used in the teaching process. When they are learning the names of places, colors, days of the week, flowers, and the like, they can use these words in repeated patterns or in interesting combinations. Complex or unusual rhythms should not be avoided if they are present in normal speech patterns and already somewhat familiar to the child. Children are flexible enough to adapt readily to changing meters and polyrhythms, and can accept them as naturally as they do the more traditional rhythmic patterns. When the teacher presents word-rhythms in notation, care must be taken that these rhythms are represented with precision. However, care also should be taken not to distort the inherently rhythmic nature of speech into ill-conceived durational notation. In repeated chanting, clapping or tapping, singing, and playing of rhythms that were introduced through speech, the teacher must be sure that a given rhythm pattern is performed with consistent accuracy. This should not preclude experimentation to discover alternative rhythmic possibilities.

While the children are studying rhythmic concepts through speech, other essential ideas may be introduced through the same medium. Phrasing, dynamic qualities, staccato, and legato may be discovered in this way. Emerging understandings of musical form—repetition, contrast, specific simple binary, ternary, and rondo forms—also can be developed through speech activities. Some concepts that would be quite difficult when encountered for the first time in a musical setting where melody, dynamics, and other musical events occur simultaneously, can be introduced more successfully through word rhythms that are then transferred to the musical context. Rhythmic concepts are reinforced by combining speech patterns with body rhythms—clapping, stamping, finger snapping, and *patschen* or knee-slapping. In the following example, the eighth-note pattern to be clapped by Group I might be introduced through the rhythm of the word "forbidden."

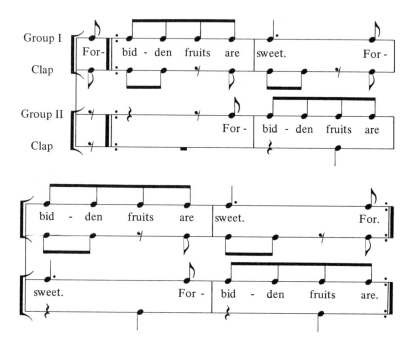

From Carl Orff and Gunild Keetman, *Music for Children, Volume I: Pentatonic,* English adaptation by Doreen Hall and Arnold Walter (Mainz: B. Schott's Sohne, 1960), p.73. Used by permission of Belwin-Mills Publishing Corp.

# SINGING

Speech, chant, and song are all points along a single continuum. Singing experiences follow directly from speech: thus, melody grows out of rhythm. The child chants single words, phrases, and nursery rhymes. He claps their rhythm patterns and plays them on instruments. He discovers that his voice rises and falls in pitch as he chants. At this point the transition is made from speaking to singing. From then on, speech and song reinforce and complement each other in the learning experience.

The earliest experiences in singing resemble play: children call back and forth, singing each other's names. Call-and-response games and songs based on counting-out rhymes develop. The teacher joins in and uses these activities to build concepts. She sings a musical phrase and the children learn by imitation. She encourages a singing dialogue and notates the sounds children make in calling to each other. These sounds are played on the tuned instruments and become materials for creative work. Practice in speaking, chanting, and clapping word rhythms prepares the child for the experience of combining these rhythms, by now familiar to him, with melody. The earliest songs in *Music for Children* illustrate the meaning of Orff's term, elemental music. They are rudimentary with the natural, singsong style children use. The following example from the supplementary material in Volume I shows how word rhythms become a basis for musical rhythm; how natural pitch inflections develop into the simplest kind of melody; how the universal "sol-mi" (5-3) chant of childhood becomes a rudimentary song; and how the words of a song relate to familiar occurrences in daily life.

Go to bed, Tom, Go to bed, Tom, Tired or not, Tom, Go to bed, Tom.

"No. 8" from Carl Orff and Gunild Keetman, *Music for Children, Volume I: Pentatonic,* English adaptation by Doreen Hall and Arnold Walter (Mainz: B. Schott's Sohne, 1960), p.92. Used by permission of Belwin-Mills Publishing Corp.

From the first page onward, songs in *Music for Children* are scored for accompaniment by instruments or by body rhythms or both. There are instrumental compositions without any vocal parts, but aside from simple chants like the one above, there are no songs without accompaniment or independent instrumental parts. There is a strict, preplanned sequence for the introduction of melodic intervals. Singing begins with the descending minor third, sol-mi (5-3). Other tones are added in the following order: la, re, do (6, 2, 1), (to complete the pentatonic scale), and then fa and ti (4, 7).

The pentatonic mode is used because Orff believed it to be the native tonality of children. In keeping with his theory that the course of music history is relived in the development of each individual, he considered the pentatonic mode appropriate to the mental development of the young child. In this mode children can improvise several melodic lines at the same time without dissonance and with less pulling toward the tonal center than in major and minor keys. In some systems the major scale is the beginning point in teaching melody. In the Orff sequence of instruction, major and minor scales are postponed until later, when they are explored extensively. A corollary to the development of a child's natural expressions is an appreciation for many kinds of tone relationship. Modes and non-Western scales can be as natural to him as the diatonic system. Likewise, his own choice of chord progressions may go beyond those admitted in traditional Western music. Exposure to such sound relationships will contribute to the development of a greater melodic and harmonic sensitivity, which will find its full release in improvisation. The child will be prepared to accept and enjoy contemporary as well as traditional music.

"The Day Is Now Over" (see page 75) is a typical example of Orff's pentatonic songs. It also illustrates several other characteristics of his instructional music. Ostinato patterns, used so extensively in these pieces, help to develop linear thinking and independence in performing one of the parts in an ensemble. The combination of several ostinatos is a frequently used device, involving several players in addition to the singers, and encouraging ensemble playing. Orff has used the simplest of motives, extracted from the melody itself, to create the introduction and the accompaniment. He intended that students create their own settings in much the same way. Like most of his instructional songs, this one appears in a complete and symmetrical setting with introduction and accompaniment. (Many of the songs also have codas.) The mood, a delicate quality that pervades Orff's instructional repertoire, is shown in the orchestration and reflects the meaning of the words. Bordun accompaniments are used extensively because their open fifths, like the droning of a bagpipe, sound well with pentatonic melodies. These drone basses become good accompaniments to improvised melodies as well. The bordun tones also begin to suggest tonal center relationships. In some *Schulwerk* compositions both tones of the bordun move up or down together. By means of embellishment or melodic figuration using neighboring tones, ostinato patterns develop out of borduns.

# MOVEMENT

Movement in the Orff approach begins with elemental movement—

the kind of movement children have without any special training. It develops, without any help, out of itself. The child likes to run, jump, skip, turn and to do many other things without any purpose; just for fun. So, he is able to create his own kind of movement which is mostly full of lively expression. The child in the first few years is not as able to express his thoughts and feelings by word as he is in movement or painting.[4]

Elemental movement is made up of untrained, natural actions, common to all children. The enjoyment of this movement parallels the child's enjoyment of making his own music in his own way. Such movements as running, skipping, turning, hopping, and jumping—often thought of as play—are part of musical development in the Orff plan. The teacher encourages these movements, relates them to music, and uses them in building musical concepts. According to Dorothee Guenther, small children everywhere enjoy and explore movement for its own sake. There is much rhythmic activity without apparent purpose when the child is left alone. He hops over imaginary obstacles, runs a few steps and stops abruptly, walks on tiptoe, and whirls until he is dizzy. These, she states, are valid ways of expressing feelings and of discovering the possibilities of creative movement. Unfortunately, they are usually stifled in early childhood.[5] Such activities are part of the concept of elemental movement. In the teaching process, the freedom and joy of exploring movement should be preserved. Movement and improvisation will foster greater self-awareness and help the child to actualize his expressive potential. And the development of perception will not only contribute to a firm foundation in music education, but also will provide the roots for a life of aesthetic education.

Several uses of movement develop on the basis of these early, spontaneous play activities. Children select patterns in movement and perform them as part of a composition they are singing and playing. Free, interpretive movement is performed by one child, or a few, or an entire group. Several songs in the five volumes of *Music for Children* lend themselves to creative dramatization, and some are linked with instrumental pieces that could well accompany dancing. The four body rhythms (clapping, stamping, finger-snapping, and *patschen*) serve several purposes. They provide a way for children to sense rhythms through movement in addition to hearing them; they are used extensively to accompany singing and chanting; and they give practice in performing rhythms, developing skill that is then transferred to the playing of special percussion instruments. Through body rhythms and in other movement, the basic concepts of musical form may be introduced. A pattern of clapping and stamping, for example, can become a theme. It can be repeated, varied, performed backward, performed antiphonally, or used as the basis for a rondo.

The body rhythms may be used by one group to accompany a poem or jingle. They may be transferred to unpitched instruments. As you see, the child begins with rhythms he has experienced in speech and melodies he has used in play. Orff fuses music with the spoken word and movement, and meets the child on his own ground.[5]

In the teacher training program, the Orff Institute at Salzburg offers five different courses in movement. In European classes generally, movement has been a more integral part of *Schulwerk* than it has been in the United States.[7] However, American proponents of *Schulwerk* are beginning to realize more and more the basic importance of movement. Movement in Orff *Schulwerk* is derived from Dalcroze Eurhythmics, but unlike Eurhythmics, it is not the central focus through which all or most musical study is approached. Children do use dance movement to interpret in their own ways the music they hear; they learn specific exercises in which they use ropes, balls, and other objects; introductions of specific rhythm patterns, tempos, and dynamic qualities are made through movement; and children have opportunities to improvise increasingly complex movements in response to music.[8]

# IMPROVISATION

The primary purpose of music education, as Orff sees it, is the development of a child's creative faculty which manifests itself in the ability to improvise. This cannot be achieved by supplying ready-made and usually much too sophisticated material of the classical variety, but only by helping a child to make his own music, on his own level, integrated with a host of related activities. Speaking and singing, poetry and music, music and movement, playing and dancing are not yet separated in the world of children, they are essentially one and indivisible, all governed by the play-instinct which is a prime mover in the development of art and ritual. We find close parallels to this in archaic cultures and in the so-called primitive stages of our own civilization. It has been suggested, that much of children's pleasure in nursery tales may arise "from an unconscious sympathy between the child and the thought and custom of the childhood of civilization." Nursery rhymes and tales have been discovered to be of incredible antiquity; not a few date back to prehistoric times. What are their musical equivalents? It is from this point of view that we shall recognize the value of repetitive patterns, which correspond to the endless repetitions in songs and tales and singing games; that we shall understand the insistence on pentatonic tunes (which represent the deepest layer of folksong) and on the primary importance of Rhythm: motor impulses manifested themselves earlier, and are still stronger, than melodic impulses.[9]

In Orff *Schulwerk*, creativity most often takes the form of improvisation. Active participation as a member of a performing group is part of the Orff concept of elemental music. The student is expected to improvise freely: this is a consistent practice in Orff classes. All the activity areas within *Schulwerk* are media for improvisation—movement, speech, body rhythms, singing, nonmelodic and melodic instruments. The instruments especially are used for improvisation. Students create rhythmic and melodic patterns, accompaniment figures,

Dalton School, New York City. Performance at 1970 White House Conference on Children.

introductions, and codas for songs. The Orff instruments lend themselves to improvisation in the classroom. Orff's followers do not expect the masterful improvisation of a trained musician: the goal of extemporaneous performance is rather to form the habit of thinking creatively. The compositions Orff wrote for children's classes are intended to serve as models for children's own innovative work today, as when he wrote them. Using these songs as models, students often choose melodic or rhythmic motives from other familiar songs and use them in creating accompaniments, introductions, codas, or variations. To encourage creativity on the part of each child, the teacher provides conditions and opportunities for improvisation. Instead of suggesting musical materials and what to do with them, he allows the students to determine the form and content of the composition they are creating. Children find genuine satisfaction in manipulating musical materials. They are expected not to be content with their initial products in improvisation. Leaders in the Orff method encourage self-evaluation, experimentation, and critical listening when children are improvising. Careful listening and a degree of aesthetic judgment are developed in this process. It is important that each child have opportunities to improvise, often using the special instruments, and to evaluate what he has produced.

Beginning with simple experiences related to play, improvisation continues throughout the instructional sequence. *Schulwerk* provides models. As children build their improvisations in the style of *Schulwerk* models, they use the compositional devices Orff suggested: bordun and ostinato, for example. A favorite simple form for improvisation is the rondo, because its structure becomes a useful framework, with the theme performed as a set pattern for all, alternating with contrasting improvisatory episodes by individuals. The instruments the children use were chosen or designed with improvisation, as a learning process, in mind. The timbres blend well and the instruments offer an interesting range of possibilities for playing the types of musical patterns on which improvisation, in this method, is based. "Sleep, Baby, Sleep" shows some of the

fa-ther guards the sheep.  Thy   mo-ther shakes the dream-land tree And

from   it  fall sweet dreams for  thee.   Sleep,  ba-by, sleep!   Thy

large stars are the sheep, The wee stars are the lambs I guess, The

fair moon is the shep-her-dess: Sleep, ba-by, sleep! The

large stars are the sheep.

Sleep, ba - by, sleep, Down

"No. 1, Sleep, Baby, Sleep" from Carl Orff and Gunild Keetman, *Music for Children, Volume II: Major: Bordun*, English adaptation by Doreen Hall and Arnold Walter (Mainz: B. Schott's Sohne, 1960), pp. 4-6. Used by permission of Belwin-Mills Publishing Corp.

ways in which musical ideas are used in the model *Schulwerk* pieces, with the goal of helping children to create their own songs. The vocal line is presented first in unison, then in thirds with the melody on top, and finally in sixths with the melody as the lower line. The thirds for alto glockenspiel suggest a rocking motion well suited to the words.

# INSTRUMENTS

Special instruments are a distinctive feature of Carl Orff's instructional approach, distinguishing it from other methods. Emphasis on rhythm as the strongest of the constituent elements of music led to the development of the specially designed percussion instruments. With the cooperation of experts in the history and building of musical instruments, Orff developed an instrumental ensemble of mellow, delicate timbre (see the reprinted article "The Schulwerk—Its Aims and Origins" by Carl Orff, page 152). The instruments are simple to play, are of excellent quality, and are more closely related to primitive models or to the instruments of non-Western cultures (such as the Indonesian gamelan) than to the percussion section of the modern symphony orchestra. The instruments are soprano, alto, and bass xylophone; soprano and alto glockenspiel; and soprano, alto, and bass metallophone. All are played with mallets. There is a wooden resonating chamber on each instrument, and tone blocks can be removed to create specific scale patterns. The instruments most commonly used in the elementary classroom are diatonic with extra blocks for F-sharp and B-flat, thus making available three major and three minor keys. Chromatic instruments of the same type also are available. Orff chose the viola da gamba and lute to supplement the percussion set. The cello and guitar can be substituted. Recorders also are used with the Orff instruments. Other instruments, such as drums, cymbals, and triangles can be used in the ensemble. *Schulwerk* does not make use of the piano as an accompaniment for singing, but tones of the piano used sparingly are effective in the ensemble sound. Addition of full piano, chord organ, or any other instrument with penetrating or contrasting timbre would destroy the intended sound. The timbre was deliberately planned for the model compositions in *Schulwerk*. Orff's followers make it clear that the instruments are not toys. Their chief advantages are their timbres, singly and in ensemble, and their appropriateness for children in the early stages of musical experience. They are designed to require only large-muscle movements, but they do require some playing technique. It is part of the *Schulwerk* plan that children be taught to play the instruments correctly.

Today the Orff instruments, well-known in a number of countries, are considered indispensable to his educational method. Orff expected the instruments he designed or chose to be used consistently throughout the *Schulwerk*. Many of the teaching techniques in this educational plan are dependent upon the instruments. Asking children to create music becomes more practical when the instruments are available. Playing instruments allows the child to state his musical ideas less selfconsciously than if he were singing them. The instructional plan includes playing solos and playing in ensemble, and alternating the two. Children can play rhythmic and melodic figures and learn to manipulate them in many ways. By playing instruments, children can participate in ensembles and begin to understand such musical principles as polyphony.

Children should always play from memory—only this will guarantee a maximum of freedom—but notation should not be disregarded; on the contrary, it should be introduced right at the beginning (together with speech-patterns for which rhythmical notation is sufficient) so that the child may jot down any rhythmical or melodic idea that occurs to him.[10]

Playing one of the specially designed instruments from memory is considered far more suitable for the young child than the study of piano or any of the instruments that require simultaneous reading of musical notation, familiarity with the nature of the instrument, and the complex process of

Canon   A canon for glockenspiels. The instrumentation may be varied.

"No. 40" from Carl Orff and Gunild Keetman, *Music for Children, Volume I: Pentatonic,* English adaptation by Doreen Hall and Arnold Walter (Mainz: B. Schott's Sohne, 1960), p.55. Used by permission of Belwin-Mills Publishing Corp.

performance. Orff's plan that the child learn from the beginning to play from memory frees him from the demands of concurrent playing, reading notation, and coordinating his performance with that of others. Notation is read from the early stages of the course, but is introduced when it is needed as a means of storing and communicating musical ideas. In the traditional study of music, memorization is a culminating activity. In the Orff approach, singing and playing are not dependent on musical scores, and memorizing is a natural beginning skill. Children use imitation, improvisation, and other creative techniques in addition to reading notation. The private study of piano and orchestral or band instruments is postponed in the Orff philosophy until the child has acquired a backlog of musical concepts in addition to certain skills.

Beginning with the simplest elements, and using performance as a mode of learning, Orff's plan leads to the playing of some challenging music. This canon shows that Orff has avoided drill and exercises as such, substituting a miniature composition. Its simple individual parts add up to an interesting whole. It is one of the culminating experiences in Volume I of *Music for Children.*

# HISTORICAL DEVELOPMENT

Orff became involved with music education during the 1920s, when Emile Jaques-Dalcroze was making his startling innovations in the field. He was influenced by Dalcroze's thinking and by the same factors that had helped to shape it: the possibility of breaking away from the traditional methods and materials of the conservatory style of music education, a surge of interest in physical training and gymnastics, and the appearance of a new kind of dancing that has since become known as modern dance. The two men shared an interest in the theater, and Orff worked in the opera houses of Mannheim and Darmstadt. In this period a number of schools for training in gymnastics and dance were opened. Orff's *Guentherschule,* founded in 1924 in Munich in collaboration with Dorothee Guenther, was unlike most schools in that its purpose was to combine the study of music with the study of gymnastics and dance. This unification of movement and music was the key to Orff's concept of music education. His years of teaching experience confirmed the inseparable nature of music and dance, and culminated in an instructional approach based on his theory of elemental music. His students at the *Guentherschule* were not, as a rule, preparing for careers in music. Most of them were amateurs in music, preparing to become teachers of physical education. Orff was challenged by the need to begin their training with the simplest rudiments. He was in an excellent position to experiment with materials and methods of his own devising. *Schulwerk* began as a practical classroom approach to the elements of music. Teaching in the *Guentherschule*, Orff sought the earliest and most basic learning experiences within the art. In 1930 the first edition of *Schulwerk*, called "Rhythmic and Melodic Exercises," was published. Like many other educators, Orff wrote his books as a means of storing and preserving ideas created in the teaching process that might otherwise be overlooked or forgotten. In World War II the *Guentherschule* and the special instruments were

Courtesy Magnamusic-Baton, Inc., St. Louis.

destroyed. Orff's work as an educator was temporarily suspended. In 1948 Orff was asked to produce the same type of music that had distinguished the *Guentherschule*, this time for a series of educational broadcasts on Bavarian radio. He revised his educational plan, originally intended for the training of physical education teachers, with new focus on the needs and abilities of children. From this time he began to formulate more clearly the elemental music. The broadcasts continued for five years. Experimental courses with children were begun at the *Mozarteum* in Salzburg. Soon the Orff *Schulwerk* had become a regular part of the curriculum there, with Gunild Keetman as teacher. Salzburg became a headquarters for *Schulwerk*, and its inclusion in the program there was an important step in the spread of the method to other countries. Today the Orff Institute, established in Salzburg in 1963, offers training in the method for teachers from many parts of the world.

In recent years an Orff-Schulwerk Association has been formed in the United States, with headquarters at Ball State University at Muncie, Indiana. The association's official bulletin, the *Orff Echo*, was first published in November 1968. Other publications, such as Orff Institute yearbooks, are published in Germany. Leaders in the dissemination of Orff's ideas were Doreen Hall and Arnold Walter of Canada, Daniel Hellden of Sweden, and Minna Lange of Denmark. Other educators took the method to Belgium, England, Greece, Holland, Israel, Latin America, Portugal, Spain, Turkey, the United States, and Yugoslavia. After 1953 Naohiro Fukui began to use the method in Japan. Simple translation of the Orff materials was not considered practicable. Orff had based his approach originally on the folklore and music of childhood that were indigenous to Germany. In order for new editions in Swedish, Flemish, Danish, French, Portuguese, and Spanish, as well as English, to be truly in keeping with Orff's philosophy, the children's lore of each culture had to be used within the *Schulwerk* plan. These developments made new editions of *Schulwerk* necessary. Today the Orff *Music for Children* is available in the English-language adaptation by Doreen Hall and Arnold Walter, in five volumes, plus a teacher's manual. In this version, some of Orff's original texts are translated, others are replaced with Mother Goose rhymes and folksongs.

Volume I     Pentatonic
Volume II    Major: Bordun
Volume III   Major: Triads
Volume IV    Minor: Bordum
Volume V     Minor: Triads [11]

There are several basic questions for American educators who are considering whether to adopt the Orff approach as wholly as possible or to adapt its principles and techniques. Orff himself seems to think that the philosophy and most of the techniques could be used in virtually any country. The materials, however, are so closely related to the stories, poems, games, and songs of childhood in a particular culture that to adopt them without change seems inappropriate. Leading *Schulwerk* teachers have studied the principles and the teaching techniques, and then have shaped the instructional repertoire from materials that were suitable for a particular nationality. Since Orff made extensive use of songs in the pentatonic mode for the first portion of the course, and this mode was so closely related, in his opinion, to the musical life of the young child, it seems logical to collect songs in the pentatonic mode and use them in Orff-inspired teaching. Those with extensive experience in teaching *Schulwerk* suggest that American folk music includes many pentatonic songs and singing games.

Some American teachers have tried combining Orff *Schulwerk* with Kodaly's Sol-fa Teaching. Denise Bacon has described her experiences in using these ideas in combination.[12] In a sense, the question of whether to combine the two approaches is an academic one. They are interrelated already, because the leaders of each movement have visited and learned from each other, as Wilhelm Keller has pointed out.

It may be interesting to get a short history of contacts between Hungarian colleagues and co-workers of Kodaly and the Orff Institute;

further to come to know what the difference is between Orff-Schulwerk and the "Kodaly method." In the last year of Kodaly's life the
Orff Institute was able to establish and foster contact with him and
a few of his colleagues—Gabor Friss, Dr. Josef Peter, Dr. Otto Borhy,
Istvanna Gaal, Katalin Forrai and others. The first meetings with
Hungarian music pedagogues during the annual "Week's Conference
on Music Education" in Graz, Austria, in which Dr. Hermann Regner and I took part, followed the ISME Conference in Budapest where
I gave a lecture on fundamental music education and its significance
as an introduction to modern music. After this lecture I had a dialogue with Zoltan Kodaly concerning the Orff-Instruments. Kodaly
told me that he had bought a collection of Orff-Instruments for a
school in a Hungarian town and that he liked the sound of xylophones more than the sound of glockenspiels. In 1965 followed a
visit by Dr. Regner and Professor Waldmann of Trossingen to learn
about the practice of music teaching according to Kodaly's ideas in
Budapest.[13]

Like Kodaly, Orff planned to teach a vocabulary of rhythmic
and melodic motives. Their techniques for doing so were
quite different, and certainly they differed in their philosophical reasons for building such a vocabulary. Kodaly
valued the repertoire of musical motives as a means of developing skill in music reading; Orff saw in such a repertoire
the means of cultivating creativity.

Criticisms of the Orff instructional repertoire have been
made. A number of interesting opinions have been expressed
by those who have tried the Orff principles in American
schools, and they represent opposite viewpoints. Janice
Thresher considers the songs too difficult for average children in the many schools where music classes are scheduled
for only two half-hour periods per week. She expressed the
opinion that children should not be limited to the pentatonic
mode for their song literature for an entire year, which she
states is the standard Orff practice.[14] Ruth Pollock Hamm,
however, declared that such a time span for using pentatonic
songs was never specified in the *Schulwerk* teacher training
classes she attended.[15] Another writer states that the songs
are too simple for today's children, who have been exposed
to a variety of songs and commercial jingles and often can

sing more difficult songs than the ones in *Schulwerk*. Assumption that speech rhythms serve as a solid foundation for learning musical rhythms is questioned by some educators. One observer believes that the rhythms of speech and those of music are not closely related.[16] The cost and use of the instruments is a controversial matter. Genuine Orff instruments are expensive and therefore are not available to all. On the other hand, Orff enthusiasts have pointed out the danger of spending too much time and attention on playing them, and consequently substituting the instruments for the *Schulwerk* itself. They feel that not just any song becomes part of the Orff plan because it is played on the authentic instruments. These instruments, they say, are meant solely as the means of a very personal, creative kind of musical expression and their use was intended as only one phase of an integrated musical experience.

Several experimental studies have been done on the basis of Orff *Schulwerk*. Martha Maybury Smith served as director of one such study in the Bellflower Unified School District of California.[17] A pilot program was carried out at the Middlefork School in Northfield, Illinois, in 1960.[18] Rees G. Olson in 1967 reported on his study in which the Orff method was compared with the traditional method for teaching melody.[19] Robert B. Glasgow and Dale Hamreus tested three assumptions about the use of the Orff approach in American schools. They dealt with teaching fundamentals of music to elementary students who were not grouped according to musical ability, improving pupil attitudes toward music, and selecting songs from the series books ordinarily used in American schools.[20] Jacques Schneider conducted an exploratory study at the Elk Grove Training and Development Center, Arlington Heights, Illinois. Working with adult students, he emphasized the principles of the Orff *Music for Children* and incorporated Kodaly-style hand signs (to represent scale tones) into the Orff framework. In the 1969 report he commented on the alternatives that are possible in adapting Orff's ideas to American schools. He came to the conclusion that the five-book series, *Music for Children*, must become a regular part of the required teacher-training curriculum if the Orff ideas are to be interpreted accurately and used correctly.[21] Margaret T. Siemens compared the Orff method and standard American methods of teaching music to children in Jefferson County, Colorado. She obtained positive results in "discrimination of better types of music" on the part of the children who were exposed to the Orff method.[22]

Arnold Burkart has analyzed the philosophy and classroom techniques in the Orff method and has shown the relationship between these and contemporary trends in music education. He has created "an operational construct" in which he shows how Orff *Schulwerk* contributes to the development of musicality. This includes teaching basic concepts of musical style and using a number of classroom activities such as speech, movement, dramatization, and playing instruments.[23] In another article Burkart states that the Orff approach is indeed appropriate for today's educational scene because it is adaptable to a teaching style based on the structure of music; it is designed to maximize the discovery process; it lends itself to individualized instruction; it encourages creativity; and it permits the teacher to act as a guide rather than an authority.[24]

Orff *Schulwerk* has already been adapted for use in working with exceptional children. Orff himself explored the possibilities of *Schulwerk* in connection with music therapy. Nancy Ferguson has written about the use of the method with perceptually handicapped children, L. Birkenshaw about working with deaf children, and Judith Bevans about her work with exceptional children. Lois Mittleman has reported her experience with urban children.[25]

Since the earliest days of American public school music, terminology has been a problem. Then and now, the meaning and usage of educational terms can hamper, rather than facilitate communication. In both Dalcroze and Orff plans, there are references to the body as a musical instrument. When Dalcroze and his followers used the term, they meant that the entire body could be developed into a tool for the sensitive expression of musical feeling, and of specific musical happenings: tempo, dynamics, phrasing, and many concepts dealing with rhythm and melody. Doreen Hall, in the Teacher's Manual for Orff-Schulwerk *Music for Children,* titled one of the chapters "The Body as an Instrument." In this chapter she explained the specific body movements used to teach and reinforce rhythmic concepts: clapping, stamping, finger-snapping, and *patschen.* Orff's followers react unfavorably when their instructional work is called a system, and when terms like "fixed patterns," and "formula" are used in connection with it. They consider it a philosophical approach or a set of principles, rather than a dogmatic method. Orff himself described it as a work that is never quite finished, but is constantly changing and developing.[26] The purpose of insisting on certain terminology in this case is to avoid the impression of a closed or finished instructional system. It is important to maintain an attitude of flexibility, openness to change, and readiness for creative work.

To be sure, further development of the plan invented by Orff is possible and desirable. The various studies cited above indicate some possibilities.

Carl Orff would, I feel certain, be the first to object to defining too closely the proper modes to use and the system to follow. . . . I am sure that his greatest happiness would lie in the knowledge that his imaginative leadership has provoked the interest and desires of others to move further in the almost limitless field which lies ahead.[27]

---

[1] Carl Orff, "Orff-Schulwerk: Past and Future," *Perspectives in Music Education* (Washington, D.C.: Music Educators National Conference, 1966), p. 386.

[2] Ruth Pollock Hamm, "The Challenge of the Orff Approach for Elementary Music Education," *Musart,* Vol. 22, No. 5 (April-May 1970), p. 16.

[3] Doreen Hall and Arnold Walter, English adaptation of *Music for Children* by Carl Orff and Gunild Keetman, Volume I: Pentatonic (Mainz: B. Schott's Sohne; U.S.A. distribution, Belwin-Mills Publishing Co.), p. 92.

[4] Ursula Klie, "Principles of Movement in the Orff-Schulwerk," *Musart,* Vol. 22, No. 5 (April-May 1970), p. 42.

[5] Dorothee Guenther, "Elemental Dance," *Orff Institute Year Book 1962* (Mainz: B. Schott's Sohne, 1963), p. 37.

[6] Hamm, p. 16.

[7] Denise Bacon, "Kodaly and Orff—Report from Europe," *Music Educators Journal,* Vol. 55 (April 1969), p. 53.

[8] Klie, pp. 42-43.

[9] Arnold Walter, Introduction to *Music for Children*.

[10] Carl Orff, Introduction to *Music for Children*.

[11] Hall and Walter. See also the English adaptation by Margaret Murray (Mainz: B. Schott's Sohne).

[12] Bacon, p. 53.

[13] Wilhelm Keller, "What is the Orff-Schulwerk—and What it is Not!" *Musart*, Vol. 22 (April-May 1970), p. 50.

[14] Janice M. Thresher, "The Contributions of Carl Orff to Elementary Education," *Music Educators Journal*, Vol. 50 (January 1964), p. 43, p. 47.

[15] Ruth Pollock Hamm, "Orff Defended," *Music Educators Journal*, Vol. 50 (April-May 1964), p. 90.

[16] Marion Flagg, "The Orff System in Today's World," *Music Educators Journal*, Vol. 53 (December 1966), p. 30.

[17] "Orff-Schulwerk. . . . Innovation at Bellflower," *The Instructor*, Vol. 77 (May 1967), p. 76.

[18] Grace C. Nash, "The Orff Schulwerk in the Classroom," *Music Educators Journal*, Vol. 50 (April-May 1964), p. 92.

[19] Rees Garn Olson, "A Comparison of Two Pedagogical Approaches Adapted to the Acquisition of Melodic Sensitivity in Sixth Grade Children: The Orff Method and the Traditional Method" (Ph.D. Dissertation, Indiana University, 1967).

[20] Robert B. Glasgow and Dale Hamreus, "Study to Determine the Feasibility of Adapting the Carl Orff Approach to Elementary Schools in America" (Oregon College of Education, Monmouth, May 27, 1968), ED 020 804.

[21] Jacques Schneider, "Orff Program: Music for Children," U.S. Office of Education, Washington, D.C., July 1969), ED 037 474.

[22] Margaret T. Siemens, "A Comparison of Orff and Traditional Instructional Methods in Music," *Journal of Research in Music Education*, Vol. 17 (Fall 1969), p. 272.

[23] Arnold Burkart, "Orff-Schulwerk and the Development of Musicality—An Operational Construct," *Musart* (January 1971), p. 14.

[24] Arnold E. Burkart, "Orff-Schulwerk Related to Contemporary American Educational Thought," *Musart* (January 1971), p. 6.

[25] Nancy Ferguson, "Orff with the Perceptually Handicapped Child," *The Orff Echo*, Vol. 2 (June 1970), p. 1; L. Birkenshaw, "Teaching Music to Deaf Children," *Volta Review*, Vol. 67 (May 1965), p. 352; Judith Bevans, "The Exceptional Child and Orff," *Music Educators Journal*, Vol. 55 (March 1969), p. 41; Judith Bevans, "The Exceptional Child and Orff," *Education of the Visually Handicapped*, Vol. 1 (December 1969), p. 116; Lois Mittleman, "Orff and the Urban Child," *Music Educators Journal*, Vol. 55 (March 1969), p. 41.

[26] Carl Orff, "Orff Schulwerk: Past and Future," p. 386.

[27] Theodore Mix, "Orff Schulwerk. . . . A Means or an End?" *New York State School Music News*, Vol. 31 (January 1968), p. 35.

# PART TWO:

# THE AMERICAN CURRICULUM AND THE EUROPEAN PLANS

# THE MUSIC CURRICULUM IN THE UNITED STATES

Much of the eclecticism of American music education stems from deep within the American society. Surely no national group in the world is more widely diverse in as many ways as are the people of the United States. From the beginning, the American population was composed of groups and individuals with strong and differing characteristics. The characteristics have blended and mellowed, yet they remain. A traveler must find very striking the differences in the English language as spoken by Americans in Alabama, Texas, Minnesota, Maine, and metropolitan New York. This is but one of the evidences of cultural differences derived from the roots of three hundred years ago. Preferences in literature and the arts are as strong in many places as language differences. A child on an Arizona Navajo reservation, a Mexican-American child of New Mexico, and a San Francisco Chinese-American child will not sing the same folk songs or respond to music in the same way as a child of rural Vermont or rural Iowa. Nor will their parents be likely to have the same aspirations for arts education of their children. While in the past, especially in some periods of our history, Americans observed their old-country traditions and customs privately in their homes and neighborhoods, their attitude today is different. They often do not care to melt entirely into the image of the mythical American, but rather, they cherish their heritage and require that educators do likewise.

For generations in Germany and Hungary it has been most natural for children to begin musical experience with old, traditional folk songs of the country. Early America had no such songs, and from the beginning American children sang folk songs from the British Isles and Europe. In a nation still comparatively young, a literature of its own folk songs has developed, but often the songs are patterned after or even are based on melodies, rhythms, and texts from other places and times. A song (such as "En Roulant Ma Boule") that for one child is an oddity may be second nature for a child in another part of the country. These facts give American children a very different starting place from children of other countries and a great variety of starting places within their own country. Furthermore, the philosophy of American music educators embraces the point of view that there is an obligation to include all musics of the world as material for music education, from ancient Chinese *gagaku* and the Indian *raga* and *tala* to twentieth-century composed music. Added to the variety of ethnic, folk, and composed literature is the literature of American popular or youth music and jazz.

Environmental and cultural differences are only one of the factors that affect the building of curriculum. The individual mental and emotional makeup of children gives a music teacher a great deal of pleasure and it gives him also the challenge and necessity of finding many avenues of musical appeal. Closely related to this challenge is that of developing a program for students with highly diversified goals. For some, music will become a profession. The music teacher is constantly pressed to feel that his program will be a help and not a hindrance to the musically gifted. For most, music will be an enrichment. To be enriching in the student years and to prepare for enrichment in later life, musical experiences must be vital, genuine, personal, deep in emotional response and intellectual thought. The gamut of goals, including those of the dilettante, casual performer, professional performer, casual listener, and serious listener are included in the goals of musician-teachers working in a nation that aspires to educate all its children in all branches of human experience.

Other differences affecting curriculum in music education are those of school organization, the learning environment, and professional resources. A program designed for an urban, year-round high school from which students go directly into jobs or technical schools may be different from that designed for a rural or suburban high school. A program for an ungraded elementary school or for an open school will be somewhat different from that of a traditional school. An elementary program taught by trained music teachers who work directly with the children may not be the same as the program taught by classroom teachers. In education that encompasses all these differences in culture, locale, individual learning, diversified goals, school organization, learning environments, and professional resources, only a highly diversified curriculum can possibly function. Certainly, the differences are more numerous and more marked in the United States than anywhere else, and a chief objective must continue to be development of a diversified eclectic curriculum.

From where, then, or what, is unity derived? Certainly, fragmented and scattered plans for teaching music never can be effective. A bit of something here, an experience in something else there, in a program without design or developmental possibilities, never will result in satisfaction or the continuing, consistent growth that is essential in music education. In common practice today, the musical elements, defined in various ways, are considered to be the substance for contemplation, consideration, and analysis. The elements sometimes are defined in the general terms rhythm, melody, and harmony. From observation of these, the studies of related constituents such as dynamics and form are developed. Recently the trend with music educators is to define the elements in many terms, rather than few—terms that are less generic, more specific, and more inclusive, such as sound sources, pitch, pulse, duration, texture, dynamics, timbre, and organization. These terms are, to a greater degree, free from preconceptions and traditional meanings. Consideration of *units of pitches*, rather than *melody*, for example, makes possible analysis of the serial, chromatic, atonal, and electronic sequences of tones as well as the diatonic sequences that the term melody has come to connote. The term *sound sources* rather than *instruments* and *voices* allows for consideration of the many spoken, electronic, and concrete sounds found in contemporary music. These constituent elements, being the content of all music, become, then, the basis for study of musical sound. Whether the sound is the Indonesian gamelan, a Beethoven string quartet, drumming tunes from Ruwanda, or the latest American rock—consideration, analysis, and comparison are possible in terms of the basic elements. It is from the approach through observation and study of these elements that unity in the American music curriculum is chiefly derived.

Another curricular dimension is quite generally accepted in this country—that of the types of participation through which musical content is experienced. The three areas of experience are performing, analytical listening, and experimenting-improvising-composing. Although in many schools they are not given equal emphasis, most teachers recognize the validity and need for all three. Each area has its concomitant musical skills. Development of skill in music reading is a part of each.

*Performing*

Singing and playing music always have been and probably will continue to be the heart of the music curriculum. A major goal of American education is that every child develop his singing voice and enjoy expression in singing. Much of the curriculum in which children learn basic musical content and musical symbols stems from folk and composed songs children sing. Relatively simple melody and percussion instruments are considered to be an important part of classroom equipment. Bells, xylophones, the recorder, harmonica, Melodica, guitar, Autoharp, tambourine, drums, maracas, and a variety of other percussion instruments are commonly played by children in the elementary classroom. Opportunity to learn to play an orchestral instrument in the elementary school is a unique feature of American music education. Children in the upper age levels usually are offered lessons as a part of free public education, and sometimes instruments are furnished. Skills learned in small instrumental classes are reinforced by those learned in the general classroom. Reciprocally, young instrumentalists often play harmony parts with class singing and the class observes instruments at close range. Body movement and dance are a type of performing experience in the classroom. Primary children often have their first and most significant relationship with music as they listen and move to sounds played by the teacher on the piano, a drum, or other instrument, or on recordings. As children become aware of the musical elements, their movement is refined as realization of the music and becomes in fact a performance of it.

*Analytical Listening*

Believing that children must know a great deal of music literature beyond what they can perform, a large proportion of the curriculum is based on recorded music children hear and analyze. More or less unique to American education is the point of view that even young children should hear the greatest literature and a broad variety of it. From the beginning of their education, children hear sections of standard symphonies, concertos, sonatas, and vocal works, as well as ethnic, electronic, and many other types of contemporary music. The biggest and most complex sounds are considered appropriate for children's listening. It is believed that general aesthetic experience is valuable and that intellectual analysis follows rather than precedes this experience. Primary children may dance with music they hear, play simple instruments with it, or discuss the more obvious elements. Older children will be expected to notice more of the details and to learn relationships. They may play motives on instruments or sing them. They may analyze verbally or through movement. Experience with a large repertoire of many types of music of all eras and cultures is expected to accumulate as a part of elementary education.

*Experimenting-Improvising-Composing*

The most generally accepted theory of American music education today is that students should discover musical principles through their own exploration and manipulation of sound. Teachers attempt to provide an environment in which children may experiment singly and in small groups with instruments, sung and spoken words, and tape recorders. Projects are initiated through which children explore sound sources, develop original patterns of sound, and discover and apply compositional principles. Problems of notation are discovered as children devise symbols for the sounds in their compositions. Such projects are important in the study of musical elements and structures and they have important value in building attitude toward less creative experiences. A child who has developed his own theme and variations will have deeper interest in those of Beethoven. A child who has just engaged in a do-it-yourself project will be likely to give contented attention to less active music projects.

American music educators have one goal that permeates all others—that of making school music a joyous experience. Many educators, including administrators, depend upon the music experience to counteract what a contemporary writer calls the "joylessness of education." Most teachers feel that musical skills and knowledge of music cannot be well learned or applied except with pleasure. This is not to say that every moment of developing a skill will be enjoyed, but in an overall view of the experiences, enjoyment of musical sound and happiness in expression through music will prevail.

There never has been in all of history or anywhere else in the world a plan for public school music like that of present-day America. A much fuller curriculum is attempted than has been conceived in other times and places. Instrumental music is taught on a widespread basis. Every child is included in the aspiration of teachers. The fulfillment of such a plan is the enormous and often well done job of American music educators. It is in this general plan that the principles of Dalcroze, Kodaly, and Orff are being practiced in various degrees of adoption or adaptation.

# ADAPTATION:

# IMPLICATIONS AND VIEWPOINTS

Dalcroze, Kodaly, and Orff wrote music and designed their programs of instruction for particular groups of children. These groups were not small, but they were homogeneous to a degree that made it possible to fit musical content to them. The problem of adapting song repertoire to our schools has been common to all three methods. In neither case could the original song repertoire be used. Two of the basic, most common experiences of American elementary education— singing in informal groups and developing a large listening repertoire—are not part of either of the European plans. Development of hearty, joyous, informal singing of a large repertoire of songs from many places always has been a major goal of American music teachers. Often the songs are learned by rote or rote-note, and often they are sung by students in large groups in culminating experiences. And a large proportion of class music time is devoted to listening, from kindergarten through the elementary school—listening with verbal analysis, with dance, in relation to the social studies. The listening repertoire on recordings prepared for use in American schools is large, and it includes a variety of music that probably would not have been condoned by either Dalcroze, Kodaly, or Orff. The creative aspects of the American program, however, can be greatly enhanced and perhaps entirely achieved through various components of the three European plans. In the areas of developing certain musical skills and musicianship in general, many American teachers believe the European approaches to be ideal.

All three of the European innovators assumed a great deal more time than is given to music instruction in schools in the United States. Indeed, the time factor seems to be one of the most crucial in improvement of music education in this country. Many available fine courses of study can achieve most of the important goals of music educators when they are taught completely, with adequate time for comprehension and application of principles. Certainly, the present time allotment in most schools is entirely inadequate to achieve the program set forth in the preceding pages, and no instructional plan can be of much help unless there is time for teaching it.

It is with all these facts in mind that American music educators evaluate the possibilities of adopting or adapting the instructional programs outlined earlier in this book. No doubt it is for these reasons that practice of principles and adaptation of method and materials rather than full adoption has been the more general response of those who are acquainted with the European plans. Numerous institutes, associations, printed materials, and workshops in the United States present the three instructional plans and American adaptation of them.

Part Two of this book includes reprinted articles whose chief purpose is to present American adaptations that have proven successful and reprints of available published adaptations. Authors Willour, Frost, Nash, and Landis have written of experiences in American schools. Other articles further illuminate the three pedagogies and their settings—the articles by Kodaly, Kraus, Ringer, Orff, and Walter—and include implications for adaptation. Author Ling writes of a fourth instructional plan from the same part of the world. The reprinted examples of available material published in the United States are a cross-section of the materials, and are not all-inclusive. More such materials are appearing regularly from the American and English publishers.

This article, written by an instructor in music education, Cleveland State University, Cleveland, Ohio, appeared in *Music Educators Journal*, September 1969.

# BEGINNING WITH DELIGHT

Judith Willour

The primary characteristic distinguishing the Dalcroze eurhythmic method from other methods of teaching music is that it develops a feeling for an awareness of music through *body movement*. In this system of rhythmic re-education, originated by the Swiss musician Emile Jaques-Dalcroze (1865-1950), the body is actually used as a musical instrument in interpreting the sounds.

Rhythmic sense, a musical ear, the voice, and muscular coordination are developed simultaneously through various body activities. Improvised piano music is used in the classes because it can be changed to fit the child's own rhythm. Later, the child learns to adapt his rhythm to that of the music. With improvised music, there is always change; repetition occurs only when the improviser desires it. Because the music is always changing and cannot, therefore, be learned by rote, the children are forced to listen constantly. Thus, listening is of primary importance from the very first lesson. In describing the child's reaction to the Dalcroze method, Elsa Findlay, chairman of the Dalcroze Eurhythmics Department at the Cleveland Institute of Music in Ohio says:

At first the child delights in the fact that he has music to accompany his activities. Next he finds that he must make some adaptations in his movement as the music now seems to be leading him! At this very moment we have the beginnings of rhythmic growth, for the child is forced to listen in order to integrate his movement with what is happening at the piano. The transition from the free and individual rhythm to a disciplined one is a simple and engaging way to learn, and the child accepts it readily. It is so easy to listen and to learn when interest is high.[1]

One simple exercise used with beginning Dalcroze students is having the children tiptoe lightly when they hear the music and freeze in their places when they hear silence. When I first observed a class of four-year-old children doing this exercise, I thought it was a bit too elementary. However, when I experimented with this musical game myself in an inner-city first-grade class and found that many of the children were unable to differentiate between sound and silence because of lack of exposure to this type of activity and poor listening habits, I began to use this exercise constantly. Gradually the children learn (without being told directly) to keep in step with the music, to make their steps larger and heavier if the music becomes louder, to make smaller movements when the music is soft, to slow down or speed up if the tempo changes, and to have smooth motions when the music is legato and quick, light movements when it is staccato. The children become less and less dependent on copying the other children as they learn to listen more carefully. The freedom and beauty of movement and the creative way many approach their motions is delightful to see.

Progression is gradual, of course. Children might begin by bouncing a ball in rhythm. Later, two groups might act out two different rhythms at the same time. One group might be walking (quarter notes), and the other running (eighth notes). It takes control to keep from conforming to the other group's rhythm and to switch rhythms when the piano requires it. When a child is more advanced, he will learn to keep two rhythms going simultaneously. For example, he could be responding to the treble part or right hand of the piano by clapping and to the bass or left hand part with his feet.

This exercise can also be done by having the right hand respond to the treble rhythm and the left hand to the bass rhythm. Children, of course, learn to analyze what they are doing and to associate the note values with their movements.

Another exercise involves passing out cards with different basic rhythm patterns to several "leaders." The children are divided into small groups so that there are three or four children with each leader. Then the various groups distribute themselves around the edge of the room (quarter notes in one corner, half notes in another).

When the piano plays one of the rhythms, the children with that particular rhythm come to the center of the room and interpret the rhythm. When the piano rhythm changes, the group in the center goes back to its place and the group representing the new rhythm enters the center.

Musical understandings that can be developed through body involvement are endless. Children can outline melody contour with their hands, bodies, or on the blackboard. They become sensitive to phrases in many ways, such as learning to change the directions of their motions at the end of a phrase. They can learn about dynamics by dramatizing a story of giants (forte—large steps) and dwarfs (piano—small steps). They can express musical form through their movements. Always, they are depicting the mood of the music. If the music is describing an airplane landing (melody contour and tempo and possibly dynamics) or a galloping horse slowing down (tempo), the child becomes the airplane or the horse, making this an even more personal experience. They enjoy using their bodies and are so involved in listening and *activity* that there is no time for misbehavior.

At the Cleveland Institute of Music most of the children begin their Dalcroze eurhythmics study when they are four years old, though there are also beginning classes for five- and six-year-olds. After two years of study, many of these children go on to theory classes, orchestral instruments, or modern dance.

Dalcroze eurhythmics is a logical place for a potential musician to begin, but it is not intended only for those who will pursue music seriously. The end results of Dalcroze exposure go beyond its musical implications. The activities can contribute to a child's total personality by encouraging imagination and creative response. Eurhythmics offers a variety of ways for a child to express himself freely and, therefore, can influence his temperament and his psychological development. By strengthening his powers of concentration

and his listening ability, as well as his ability to make musical analysis, Dalcroze develops a child's intelligence. Listening skills, which demand concentration, play a paramount
role in the growth of the child, since he must be able to listen
and hear discriminately before he can act positively.

There are other benefits to be derived from eurhythmics.
The experience of participating in this type of class-situation
helps the child adjust to other social and group situations. A
great deal of aggression and destructive emotion can be safely
expressed in socially acceptable patterns. The activities that
develop from eurhythmics help to relieve tensions and pres-
sures that occur throughout a school day. Relaxation, which
is very necessary to gain the attention and interest of children,
makes it possible to develop other areas of learning.

There would be many advantages to incorporating Dalcroze study into nursery schools and kindergartens across our
country. Children would be much better prepared to enter
their general academic studies as well as more advanced
music studies. We are told by psychologists and educators
that children with poor muscular coordination are slow learn-
ers. Dalcroze eurhythmics demands and develops coordination and encourages mastery of large muscle movements. It
stresses smooth body movement, a foundation for success in
other physical activities. It develops eye-hand-body coordination necessary in other academic subjects, such as reading.
Good listening habits, powers of concentration, and the experience of being in an organized class situation would help
all students follow teachers' directions and learn the role of
a pupil. Through eurhythmics, children learn to associate
sounds and symbols and to train their eyes to follow from
left to right. The understanding of patterns (meter) that is
developed in Dalcroze eurhythmics can be of value in later
studies of math. The ability to analyze is stressed in eurhythmics.

As with any unusual approach in teaching, there are some
difficulties to be overcome. One problem is that the music
teacher may have little skill in movement. The teacher also
may not have enough experience at the keyboard to impro-

vise. The ability to improvise at the piano should be a skill demanded of everyone who will teach music in public schools. A third problem that must be met in initiating eurhythmics classes is that of space. In order to have freedom of movement, there must be adequate room. These problems are not without solutions, and the benefit of exposing children to Dalcroze eurhythmics makes it worth working to eliminate the difficulties.

Because Dalcroze eurhythmics is a creative approach to music, each music educator can develop the concepts with variations. It can be treated as a pure subject or incorporated into an already existing music program. The aims of Dalcroze eurhythmic study are constant but the teaching methods can be very flexible. Music educators should incorporate some Dalcroze eurhythmics work in their general music program for kindergarten and primary grades and expose each child to as much of this type of training as possible.

Too often music is taught by drilling facts and theory into children rather than by arousing their interest so that they want to learn more about music. Certainly, music can and should at times be an academic discipline, especially in upper grades. However, enjoyment of music and a serious, academic study of it are not mutually exclusive. Emile Jaques-Dalcroze himself believed that the most important effect of music study should be an awakening of a love for the art in the pupil. Dalcroze eurhythmics is an example of an approach to music that is serious and yet at the same time can be thoroughly enjoyed by all participants. If more music were taught with this philosophy, our schools would produce many more music enthusiasts as well as serious musicians.

---

[1] Elsa Findlay, "Dalcroze," *Children and Music,* special compilation from *The Instrumentalist,* p. 24.

The author of this article is Secretary-General of the national music education organization in Germany and is well-known in music education throughout the world. He was a close friend and colleague of Kodaly. His article is a quite comprehensive overview with special value for the description of Kodaly's publications. The article appeared in the fall 1967 issue of *International Music Educator.*

# ZOLTAN KODALY'S LEGACY TO MUSIC EDUCATION

Egon Kraus

Kodaly published thirty-three studies and essays which in their entirety present a complete picture of a unified concept of music education. Basic questions concerning musical education are so treated that an organic structure is recognizable in which the general and professional musical education is seen as a common entity. Through all these essays the battle against musical illiteracy runs like a red thread as a prerequisite for the erection of an independent musical culture.

*Music in the Kindergarten*

The musical education of children cannot begin early enough. In Kodaly's essay "Music in the Kindergarten" (1941-1958) one can read:

"In the Kindergarten the child learns while playing. It is already too late to do this in the elementary school. The new psychology states emphatically that the age from three to seven years is much more important for education than the later years. What is spoiled or missed in these years can never be repaired or recovered again later. In these years the fate of the man is decided for his lifetime. If the soul lies fallow until the seventh year it will also be unreceptive to later sowing."

Song and play belong together for the child. "The simple song does not hinder the action of play, rather the opposite; it makes play more attractive, more interesting. The limited time available for musical education of the child can thus be extended on the playground without diminishing the time for other activities. The instinctive, natural speech of the child is song, and the younger the child, the more he desires to express himself in movement.

Kodaly laid the blame for the unmusical or even hostile attitude of the Hungarian society toward music on the failure of the former kindergartens and primary schools. His criticism was turned especially toward the song literature which he felt was "neither satisfactory for the national nor the general humanistic education. The poor quality of melody did not lead the children to good music but rather to musical trash. It did not develop the musical possibilities as far as the child's talents would allow."

Above all Kodaly scolds those educators who think that "a watered-down substitute of art is good enough to serve as learning material. Only the best is just good enough for children. Everything else is only damaging. No one is too great to write for children. Quite the opposite—one should strive to be worthy of this task. What is needed are original works which in text, in melody, and in atmosphere take cognizance of the child spirit and voice.

Still in 1957, Kodaly complained about the continued use of the piano in accompanying children's song and play, their rhythmic-musical exercises and even the telling of fairy tales. "When the child becomes used to seeking only and continuously for the extra-musical illustration in music he will never understand music. When a song is always accompanied the feeling for the beauty of the pure melodic line is destroyed and it is just this which should be cultivated as the primary goal."

The kindergarten age can be used throughout for playful and child-suitable work with musical elements. For such work, melodies with simple rhythms in the pentatonic area are most suitable. Such melodies should be sung by the children without texts and finally with tonic sol-fa syllables. "The ear training of children develops faster if the songs are learned through their melodic line rather than from the text."

Kindergarten and primary school teachers are usually opposed to solmisation because they themselves do not have
command of this simple system. The syllables are fun for the
child, and he masters the basis of musical thinking in a playful way through their use. "Actually there is no difficulty in
teaching six to seven year old children sol-fa singing. If they
enter school with the knowledge of sol-fa singing the singing
instruction would progress much faster."

Kodaly never gets tired of praising the advantages of the
pentatonic scale for music education in kindergarten and primary grade. "There are still too many kindergarten teachers
and others who plague little ones with songs set in a large
range and containing large intervals, and thereby endanger
the musical and vocal development of the child. A child who
is too early pressured into the use of diatonic melodies will
never learn to sing accurately in tune. A good ear will always
detect the deviations between mi and fa (the teacher who
always sings loudly with the children naturally will not hear
this even if she, by chance, sings with perfect intonation). If
however, the children have gained security in the use of the
five principal tones of the pentatonic the use and aural arrangement of the halfsteps will cause no difficulty.

At another time Kodaly states, "tonal consciousness and the
capability to sing tones correctly develops better with the use
of pentatonic melodies which mix tonal steps and leaps, than
with the diatonic tonal 'ladder-climbing'."

The pentatonic sharpens the ear, captures the attention, and
encourages tune perfection in singing. Pentatonic melodies
contain characteristic motives which make stronger impres-
sions since they function as units and are perceived as such.

Conditions are similar in the area of rhythm. Kodaly begins with simple rhythms, but these are from the very beginning characteristic and dynamic. Rhythmic life makes the perception, recognition, and memory of melodies much easier.

In place of piano accompaniment Kodaly suggests childlike percussion and barred instruments. The melody instruments (for example the cymbalon-psalter) should be penta-
tonically tuned. Every child would be able to learn the use of

these instruments very early. "In this way the invaluable pos-sibilities to do something for the musical education of the child, and at the same time to satisfy his compulsion to act, are made available."

*Music in the School*

The basis of school music education is the development and cultivation of the human voice. The music instruction in the elementary school is primarily singing instruction. "A thorough musical education is only possible where singing has been the basis. The playing of an instrument is often only possible for a few selected individuals. Only the human voice, which is a possession of everyone, and at the same time the most beautiful of all instruments, can serve as the basis for a general musical culture."

The child must learn to read notes through song before he holds an instrument in his hands. "Lucky the child who re-ceives his first associations with notation through his own singing. When he begins to sing and, at the same time, is burdened with the notions of instrument techniques he will no longer be able to recognize the vocal ideas as primary or fundamental. If he never sings at all he will achieve a free and inner music making only with great difficulty, if at all. The disadvantages of an education which is not built on song cannot be overcome even by the greatest musical gift."

Kodaly decided in favor of the relative sol-fa syllables at a very early date. Besides many other didactic considerations the most important factor in this decision was the one that the pupils would gain command over their voices through systematic solfege instruction. The goal of this instruction is that the aural and the visual picture of music should make an indivisible unit. The relative sol-fa method clarifies the rela-tionship of tones between one another, the tonal relations being easily realized and understood especially if strengthened by the use of hand signs.

The systematic solfege instruction begins in primary school, and must be continued through the highest classes of singing and instrumental playing, "until one can read notes as an

educated adult reads a book; silently, but with the most exact
and actual idea of its sound . . . One who does not hear what
he sees, and who cannot see what he hears, does not deserve
to be called a musician."

Kodaly feels that the failure of music education up to now
is due to the fact that no suitable method of elementary music
education has been used.

"A mechanical instrumental instruction, making music with
fingers only, not with the spirit, the neglect of musical basic
instruction, solfege, is the direct cause of the decline of singing and also the increase of second class professional musicians and dilettants who overestimate their own capacities."

Music education must be built on one's own musical tradition. The musical mother tongue is the foundation of musical
instruction. "Our musical education process during the last
seventy years was a mistake, and therefore it remained without success. One wanted to educate the people to music by dis-
carding all that which the people knew for themselves. But
one can build only on something that is already at hand. If we
do not build on our own musical tradition then we build on
sand."

The folk song is not the song of uneducated classes but
rather the inheritance of the people. "It is not a primitive
form, but rather the matured, clarified art resulting from
centuries of development. It is the most complete expression
of the national soul, the nucleus and basic stock of national
musical culture. The shortest way to the folk song is by way
of musical education." Obviously an organically planned
music education must go beyond the folksong. "But in order
to do this we must encompass the folksong."

Only when one's own musical tradition has become again
the national source and basis of all musical education the way
to the music of the world opens itself more and more. "We
are closer to the realization of a world music than of a world
literature that Goethe imagined. But the question is, how can
we take our place in world music more quickly; through loos-
ing or strengthening our individuality? Perhaps one would
think that we would be better musical world-citizens the more

we cultivated a world outlook and the more we neglected our own, but I believe just the opposite. The more we cultivate and study our own music the more we shall be able to contribute to world music."

Whether folk music or art music, the decisive factor for the selection is above all the artistic value . . . the level of taste. "In art bad taste is a real spiritual illness. It is the duty of the school to offer protection against this plague. The school of today does not only neglect to do this, it actually opens doors and gates to the trash of music. In school, singing and music making must be taught in such a way that in the child for all his life a desire for noble music is awakened."

Right in the beginning of school music education stands the unaccompanied single voice song. Very early, in the third class, perhaps even before capability in reading notes in the second class, Kodaly recommends the introduction of two-part singing. "Its resulting worth is invaluable, not only in respect to polyphonic hearing, but also to the perfection of one-voice singing. Singing in tune is only learnable by two-part singing. The two voices correct and balance each other."

"The simple instrumental accompaniment to unison melody develops a passable, unclear, and still insecure instinct for harmony. Polyphonic music, however, can only be perceived by our ears when we hear a different melody simultaneously, only when we have learned to sing an independent melodic line without the support of any accompaniment. In this way we come to an understanding of a musical style in which the voices do not sing only for themselves, but in which they assist and complement each other and thereby build a higher unit."

The rhythmic studies also must begin earlier and much more intensively than was formerly the case. Rhythm should likewise be studied in groups, that is, "two-voiced." The musical group study presents an advantageous educational media which the older schools unfortunately never used.

From the pentatonic two-voiced material by way of easy diatonic polyphony instruction proceeds organically to the bicinia[1] of the old masters. "From there it is but one step to the two- and more-part polyphonic music of the great masters, and the wonderful realm of vocal music reveals itself to the astonished child. To the ear developed in this manner even instrumental music will no longer be a foreign language, despite the fact that one has not learned to play an instrument."

Obviously the gifted children should start to learn the instruments which they have some talents for. Singing however is possible for all and must therefore remain the basis of musical education. In addition to the classroom chorus and the school chorus, small vocal ensembles of three and four pupils should be established. These should try to sing at sight melodies of all styles without the assistance of instruments. This can be followed by two- and three-part songs. "Nothing can stimulate the general musical perception so much as the responsibility for singing an independent part by oneself."

Music education in school is in the same way responsible for the education of the whole society as well as for the elite. Both must be given equal consideration. "The greatest mistake of our culture is that it is built from the top down, and even this we do too quickly. Culture is the result of slow development. Hurrying it unduly, or changing the order of its development is impossible. Unfortunately, we have built the highly decorated towers first. Only when we discovered that the whole building was in danger to fall down we began to bolster up the foundation walls. Even yet the foundation is not correctly built."

The training of professional musicians has its problems also, but the problem of the music education of the public has not yet even reached the level of research and experiment. It must begin in the primary school. "The goal is: To educate children in such a way that they find music indispensable to life . . . of course good artistic music."

In professional music education Kodaly strives for a connection between musical tradition and world outlook. "We must recognize all the worthwhile tradition of Western European music, but we must not educate mere Europeans but musicians who are at the same time Hungarian musicians. Only the blending of European and Hungarian tradition can achieve a result that is worthwhile and valid for the Hungarian nation. We must imbibe the Hungarian musical life through folk music if we are to compensate for the fact that it concerns itself with only a small community."

At the commemoration of the fifth anniversary of his friend Bartok's death, Kodaly put this question "How shall we evaluate his legacy? The prerequisite for a final return of Bartok is a musically educated Hungary. All the factors must work together in order to achieve this if his art should finally reach those from whom it proceeded, the working folk, and is to be understood by them. Only then will there be a Hungarian musical culture."

*Kodaly's Musical Pedagogic Publications*
*(1) Songs for little children—Fifty Nursery Songs*

Kodaly has set fifty pentatonic melodies to words by Hungarian contemporary poets who came close to his endeavors. "The Songs for Little Children are set not in a cosmopolitan speech but in Hungarian musical language." The songs are progressively arranged and do not go beyond the range of a sixth. The melodies proceed from two tones (Nos. 1-6) through three tones (Nos. 7-15), four tones (Nos. 16-34) to the full pentatonic (Nos. 35-50).

The tone do should in no way be considered the central tone of these melodies. This may be observed in the different tonal order of the three tone melodies (the tone with a line below is always the tonic or principal tone).

No. 7 m-r-*d*; No. 8 m-*r*-d; No. 9 r-d-*l*; Nos. 10-12 d-*l*,-s,; No. 13 d-l-*s*,; No. 14 *d*-l,-s,.

Songs with modal tendencies are much in the majority. Those melodies which have do as a central tonic and tend to be in major, are in the minority.

In this way the fluctuating character of the pentatonic is emphasized much more than, for example, in the melodies of the Orff Music for Children.

*(2) Pentatonic Music*

This collection comprises four books with a content of 440

pieces. The melodies are notated only by syllables. Kodaly hopes by this means to intensify the inner hearing, and to sharpen the tonal perception. The pentatonic melodies serve the teaching of perfect intonation, the development of musical perception, and the introduction to the understanding of Hungarian music.

*Volume 1:100 Hungarian Folksongs*

The range of tones is slowly broadened from the third (m-d) through the fifth (s-d), sixth (l-d; m-s,) to the octave (l-l; s-s,) to the ninth (l-s,).

This extension takes place in the course of twenty songs. The major octave range (d'-d) is first reached in Nos. 23 and 24 and immediately dropped again. At the same time a similar extension of rhythm can be observed. For the first time syncopation occurs in No. 32, and in No. 36 the typical divided rhythm.

The first 48 songs are in duple metre. Nos. 49 and 69 present complex metres for the first time, and Nos. 90, 92, 98 are in ⅝ metre.

The introduction of "rubato" (free flowing rhythm) occurs in No. 63, and "parlando" (free rhythm in accordance with speech rhythm) in No. 74.

The final quarter of the volume contains up to the last song a forceful and logical organic increase in difficulty of rhythmic complexities.

*Volume 2: One Hundred Little Marches*

Kodaly wrote these pieces in order to compensate for the lack of short folk melodies with simple rhythms in pentatonic tonality. "We need melodies for children which are in the spirit of folksongs but which lack their difficulty, and with which we can musically prepare the basis for the real folksongs."

With these melodies the children already learn some typical melodic patterns so that later they can feel at home with folksong and Hungarian music.

The 8-16 measure pieces encompass the range of the sixth, the octave, and the ninth up to the tenth. The open tonal cadences on the changing principal tone of the pentatonic scale are characteristic.

*Volume 3: One Hundred Tscheremissian Songs*

The selection and graded arrangement of the melodies bespeak the experienced and goal-conscious pedagogue, especially through the gradual increase in tonal and rhythmic difficulties.

*Volume 4: One Hundred Forty Tschuwachian Songs*

At the conclusion of Volume 4, Kodaly writes "Whoever has conquered the rhythmic difficulties of the music of the Tschuwachian, Tscheremissian, and other Eastern peoples will easily overcome the complicated rhythms of modern music. The world vista will expand more and more and the restriction to a single national musical culture will disappear. The Tschuwachian melodies contain larger rhythmic irregularities, extraordinary metres and metric changes."

*(3) Three Hundred Thirty-Three Reading Exercises—Introduction to Hungarian Folkmusic*

This Hungarian Singing Primer explores a total of twenty different tonal organizations (modi or melodic patterns) in strict pentatonic. Within each melodic grouping there is a carefully planned increase in rhythmic difficulty. Particular rhythmic tensions (as the divided rhythm), complicated metres, and metric changes appear only in the last part of the book. This whole book of instruction contains no exercise in triadic harmony, neither in major nor minor. Exercises built on do as the tonic of the pentatonic appear first in No. 325.

"We need many reading exercises in order to have notated examples at hand which are continuously new and which have never been seen before. He who can recognize the principal interval more or less well does not yet read, he only spells . . . One must read in whole concepts, first a word (motive), then more, grasp a whole phrase at once, and arrive at the details from a consideration of the whole. We should perceive the melody in its entirety before we sing it aloud."

The one-voice reading exercises can be used at every educational level as elementary material.

Kodaly recommends the following methodical procedure:

1. only clap the rhythm
2. sing the rhythm on a single tone
3. sing the melody on a syllable suitable for vocalization
4. sing the melody on sol-fa syllables

Later when the usual note names are introduced the transposition by tonic sol-fa syllables into different tonalities is possible. Rhythm should always have precedence since the main cause for bad note reading is to be found in rhythmic uncertainty.

In these melodies many descending skips are found. "Intervals are usually practiced in ascending skips even though it is much more difficult to sing them in the descending direction."

The 333 Reading Exercises build a bridge from simple pentatonic children's songs to the rhythmically and tonally rich Hungarian folksongs with their distinctive characteristics of historical generation. "It is a wrong method to begin with diatonic melodies and only to take up the pentatonic later as if to return to a strange curiosity."

*(4) Let Us Sing Correctly—Two-Part Song Exercises*

This collection contains 107 short exercises as an introduction to two-part singing. The progressively ordered melodies avoid rhythmic difficulties and, with the exception of the last two, half-tone steps, so that concentration on perfection of intonation is not neglected. In the first exercises (Nos. 1-39) only one voice moves while the other remains as a bourdon (pedal) tone.

All exercises are repeated with an exchange of melodic line between the voices. If the tonal range permits it, the same key is used, otherwise a new tonality either higher or lower.

The exercises are hummed, or sung on vocalizing syllables, or with sol-fa syllables. Every instrumental accompaniment, above all the piano, is avoided.

If at the beginning the simultaneous attack of two voices is found to be difficult, the second voice can begin one half measure later. The less lively voice should always begin, however.

"The training in perfect intonation is no superfluous pedantry. Such exercises are excellent for ear training and for richness and beauty in choral sound. Only a chorus with perfect intonation has real color and real polish. The good sound of combination tones is the proof, but at the same time the reward of correct singing." In the foreword Kodaly explains in detail the further way to diatonic two-part singing (first the introduction of fa and then of ti).

*(5) Bicinia Hungarica—Introduction to Two-Part Singing*
Volume I Nos. 1-58: 17 folksong settings and 41 original songs. Nos. 1-30 are pentatonic melodies and Nos. 31-58 are non-pentatonic with two exceptions. The melodic line is frequently exchanged between upper and lower voices. Some melodies are based on an ostinato. The rhythmic difficulties also are gradually increased in the two-part setting (syncopations, change of metres, compound metres and unusual metres 5/4 7/8).

Volume II Nos. 59-97. 26 folksongs and 12 original melodies. Nos. 59-71 are pentatonic, No. 69 is bitonal, and No. 63 has changing metres.

Volume III Nos. 101-120. There are no pentatonic songs. The collection contains 10 Hungarian folksongs, some Geneva psalms, and other spiritual songs.

Volume IV Nos. 121-180. All the melodies are pentatonic with 3 Finnish and 17 Tscheremissian folksongs.

There is no difference of style between the Hungarian folksongs and the original songs by Kodaly. He develops his individual polyphonic style, a kind of pentatonic counterpoint, completely and organically combined with the Hungarian melodies.

The 180 Bicinia should arouse the understanding for polyphony in order to lead to the beauty of polyphonic music and to the great choral works of world music literature.

The foreword indicates that Kodaly wrote these much requiring Bicinia for children, for the school. "Folkschool in

Galanta, my dear little barefooted playmates! I thought of you as I wrote these works. Your voices sounded to me through the fog of 50 years. If we years ago had learned such songs as these how different we might have formed our life in this small country. The recognition remains for those who now are starting to learn: there is not much worth in singing only for ourselves. It is much lovelier to sing together in two parts. Then the combined singing of hundreds and thousands will be unified in a great harmony."

### (6)  Little Bicinia
This is a selection from the Bicinia Hungarica.

Volume I, Nos. 1-35, contains 29 songs out of volume I, 4 out of volume II, 1 out of volume III of the Bicinia Hungarica and 1 out of another collection. Volume I contains 23 pentatonic melodies.

Volume II, Nos. 1-29, contains 7 songs from volume I, 11 from volume II, 7 from volume IV of the Bicinia Hungarica, and 1 from the Fifteen Two-Voice Song Exercises. Volume II contains 19 pentatonic melodies.

### (7)  15 Two-Part Vocal Exercises
This volume contains little inventions and a few fugal expositions. Simple pentatonic pieces (Nos. 1-5) make an easy path to expressive polyphonic two-part singing. The work is conceived, on the one hand, as a continuation of the Bicinia Hungarica and, on the other hand, as an introduction to Bertalotti's 50 Solfeggio-Exercises. The pieces of Bertalotti can be considered as having the same significance for vocal as Bach's inventions have for instrumental schooling; the gaining of ability for judging and a certainty in stylistic questions. After intensive work with the two-part singing exercises and with Bertalotti, the pupil is capable of singing the greatest choral works of world musical literature. "This knowledge and capability also leads him to the understanding of instrumental music. The singing of a Vivaldi theme, or the simple singing of the principal themes brings the individual closer to the entire work than the best formal analysis."

*(8) 22 Two-Part Vocal Exercises*

*(9) 33 Two-Part Vocal Exercises*

*(10) 44 Two-Part Vocal Exercises*

*(11) 55 Two-part Vocal Exercises*

*(12) 66 Two-Part Vocal Exercises*

The last five works continue on the way of overcoming the difficulties of polyphonic singing through the gradual and logical increase of difficulties. Introduction to chromaticism, complicated tonalities and meters, old clefs, and themes with wide range which approach instrumental proportions. The human voice is developed into an instrument which provides an approach to art music of all times. By means of artistic polyphonic singing, and simultaneously developed ear training and musical perception, the door is open to the great works of music literature even for those who do not play an instrument. "These works only fulfill their purpose when they find an echo in the souls of millions."

Vocal education through an intensive solfege study is necessary also for the instrumentalist. "We must strive for a music making that rests on the basis of singing and springs from the spirit, rather than being based on the mechanical domination of the instrument and music making only with the fingers. Thus only one can hope that the musician will 'sing' with his instrument."

The Singing Exercises are designed for the education of the musical lay person as well as the professional musician; for the general school as well as for the special music school. "We need better lay and professional musicians. What defines a good musician can be summarized in the following points: a trained ear, a trained voice, a trained intellect, a trained heart, and trained hands. All these capabilities must be developed simultaneously and always remain in balance."

In his lectures concerning the basic goals of present day music education Kodaly frequently cites from Schumann's

"Musical House and Life Rules": "The education of the ear is most important. Concern yourself very early with the recognition of tonality and tone! Concern yourself, even if you have little vocal abilities, to sing from sight without accompaniment; the sharpness of hearing will be continuously improved in this way. You must pursue this until you understand the printed page. Sing regularly in a chorus, in particular a middle voice. This will make you musical. Listen eagerly to old folksongs, they are a mine of beautiful melodies."

*(13) Tricinia*

The 29 three-part singing exercises with texts contained in this collection serve as an introduction to old and new polyphony and lead directly to the difficult choral works of Kodaly and Bartok.

No. 29 sounds like an introduction to one of Kodaly's finest choral works (The Mountain Nights).

*(14) Epigrams (without text)*

*(15) Epigrams (The same as 14, with text)*

Kodaly indicates these nine songs with piano accompaniment simply as "one voice reading exercises." Behind this indication are hidden masterworks which above all make high technical and musical demands. The song part is entirely independent of the piano accompaniment which through its modern harmony brings sharp dissonances to the vocal part.

As in the advanced two-part singing exercises the song part is here a kind of compromise between instrumental and vocal melody.

In a wider sense the fifty children and youth choruses also belong to the pedagogical works of Kodaly. Among these, folksong settings and original works are to be found. In the works of smaller range one to two melodies are set together or varied. In the larger works several melodies are bound together to a whole. The major-minor tonalities are almost entirely avoided. Pentatonic and modal melodies dominate. Simple forms are in the majority in these children choruses.

Through relationships of the fifth, through imitation, and canonic-like voice leading a linear style is developed as an introduction to greater polyphony.

In the children's choruses by Kodaly there are devices which are related not only to the choral settings but also to the simple piano pieces of Bartok. In Bartok's as well as in Kodaly's pedagogical works one finds a "unity of pedagogic value and art value" displayed. In comparison to Bartok and Hindemith, and also to the great "pedagogic" composers of the past centuries the systematic and consistent musical didactic thinking and concern is convincing. For over 40 years Kodaly continuously enriched the music education of our times with theoretic, organizational, and practical compositional works.

Kodaly's educational reform plans and their actual realization in the music education of Hungary give again evidence of a systematic construction. The public school system and music school organization of Hungary are similarly structured of three levels: the elementary (Folk) schools correspond to elementary musical schools—the high schools (Gymnasium) correspond to conservatories of music—the university corresponds to the state academy of music.

In the eight years general elementary school music instruction for two hours per week is compulsory for all classes. A special type of elementary school, the musical elementary school, with a normal academic course of study and intensified music program consisting of a daily music class of one hour guarantees the discovery and promotion of the musically gifted youth. Each of the six conservatories is connected to a special high school for music. Besides the normal elementary school and the musical elementary school, there are special elementary music schools devoted entirely to musical training, with a one year basic course and six years of further musical training. These schools prepare the gifted child for the conservatory. The conservatory educates in a five year program, choral singers and orchestral musicians (professional musicians), and prepares students for the state academy.

Every primary school teacher for the first four classes of the elementary school receives a many-sided musical training in a teachers' training school which also includes the learning of a required instrument.

In the upper grades of the elementary school, classes 5-8, a music specialist teaches. His study includes one principal instrument, music theory, music history, composition, teaching methods and practice. Those who have been trained in the conservatories for the elementary music school can also serve as special music teachers in all public elementary schools.

In the study program for music teachers in high schools who are trained at the state academy, there is a special emphasis on vocal training and choral directing, besides the normal courses of study. The study of folkmusic is an obligatory subject for all students of the conservatory and academy.

The Hungarian teacher training system (also in the area of music) allows for an easy transfer from one level of instruction to another. Teachers trained for one type of school, i.e. elementary school, may take supplementary studies and become teachers in the high school. Such transfer facilitates professional careers.

But all these organizational efforts alone would not have been sufficient to achieve a general reform of music education in Hungary. Just as important were the didactic discussions in manifold reports and the publications of musical teaching material which, after 1937, led to an inner reform.

Within 30 years, Kodaly published 16 teaching works which in the whole present a complete music method based on singing and ear training. These publications—among them 6 collections of several volumes each with over one hundred exercises—include all levels of musical education from the kindergarten to the music academy, from the classroom choir of the primary school to the music academy choir, from the post-school singing group to the efficient amateur choir. Together with some 50 pieces for children and youth choirs the 16 pedagogical works of Kodaly comprise a comprehensive music pedagogic teaching work which makes possible an organic introduction to the choral compositions of Kodaly and

Bartok and to the large choral works of world musical literature. What Bartok achieved in the instrumental area—a
music-pedagogic microcosm—Kodaly achieved in the vocal
music area. His exemplary vocal works are not only micro-
cosmic patterns of his own style and therefore bridges to his
complete oeuvre, but at the same time provide patterns for
improvisation and invention which may build a bridge to
modern music.

---

[1] Bicinia: two-voiced songs by composers of the Renaissance period.

Zoltan Kodaly's ideas expressed in this article may be controversial among educators in the United States, but most teachers will want to give consideration to them in the context of today's teaching problems. The article appeared in *Music Educators Journal*, March 1967.

# FOLK SONG IN PEDAGOGY

Zoltan Kodaly

The Hungarian people have provided one of the best examples of how to use folk songs for educational purposes. The natural life of village people, flourishing as it did up to the First World War, was always accompanied by music and dance. Little children as soon as they began to speak, or even before, warbled ditties which they learned, however inaccurately, from their seniors. As they grew they gradually acquired all songs suitable to their age. In church they joined the community, learned the hymns by ear and, before adulthood, collected a substantial repertoire of songs. All children practiced dancing; their games began with dance-rounds. One could have observed adult people teaching the secrets of man's dancing to five-year old boys.

In more recent times, with the growth of towns and cities, children were deprived of the natural musical spontaneity that flourished in the villages. Nor was the kindergarten able to provide the musical orientation found in natural village life. Today, as the old-style life undergoes radical changes and even villages have kindergartens, these schools must perpetuate musical traditions if they are to survive.

Obviously, all reasonable pedagogy has to start from the first spontaneous utterances of the child, rhythmic-melodic expressions with repeated simple phrases which slowly give way to more complex structures. Since children learn most easily between the ages of three and six, the kindergartens would be able to accomplish much more in music if they would observe this pedagogic principle.

The fortunate child who can take part in singing games,

whether in kindergarten or in free play with other children, has a great advantage over those who never had an opportunity to do so. The elementary school should carefully examine whether or not the child has had this advantage. If not, the school has the duty to provide it, for without this foundation, no further progress is possible. Thus elementary schools first have to recapitulate the material of the kindergarten, such as singing games and rhythmical plays connected with physical movements, preferably in close cooperation with physical training. This foundation may vary with different peoples, although if one runs through the first volume of *Corpus Musicae Popularis Hungaricae*, containing children's games, he will find many international motives which verify the unity of mankind. However, since the singing games of every country are strongly dependent on their respective languages, even they are colored with nationalistic tradition.

The next step would be the folk song. Each nation has a rich variety of folk songs suitable for teaching purposes; if selected in a graded order, they furnish the best material to introduce musical elements so that the student will be conscious of them. Surprisingly quick results can be obtained by having the student sing by ear, then take dictation from the teacher. It is essential that the material used should be musically attractive. In some countries that still use the unpopular, dry, and lifeless exercises, the children grow to hate the music lesson. Incidentally, at least two lessons weekly are imperative. No result is to be hoped for if the children do not await the music lesson with thrilled expectation. If they do not feel refreshed by an exciting lesson, all labor is lost.

In Hungary, singing in elementary schools has been compulsory since 1868. Even so, as a consequence of bad teaching, many people have finished school with a hatred of music. Only the last few decades have improved the teacher's training so that tolerable results can be obtained, even with two weekly lessons. After 1945, we were able to initiate experimental schools with daily singing lessons. The results were surprising and convincing. The surplus of four hours is not an overburden; on the contrary, the progress in every other subject became easier and quicker. I dare say we may attribute this result mostly to the folk song, which is our chief material. Folk songs offer such a rich variety of moods and perspectives, that the child grows in human consciousness, and feels more and more at home in his country.

After exhausting the national treasure of rhythm and melody, foreign folk songs are the best way to introduce other types of music. As in the teaching of languages, the beginning must be unilingual. Afterwards, it should be enlarged, first by neighboring or related music and later by music of more distant peoples. Thus we are by no means chauvinistically limited to the Hungarian folk song. To become international we first have to belong to one distinct people and to speak its language properly, not in gibberish. To understand other people, we must first understand ourselves. And nothing will accomplish this better than a thorough knowledge of one's native folk songs. Later, he may proceed to comprehend other people through their folk songs.

The final purpose of all this must be to instill in the pupils the understanding and love of the great classics of the past. These are much nearer to the folk song than is generally recognized, for direct expression and clear form are common in folk songs. Haydn, the best master with whom to begin, has salient connection with folk songs. Even in many works of Mozart there is the sublimated Austrian folk song which is easy to recognize. Beethoven, as well, wrote many themes that were folklike.

The playing of instruments facilitates much musical learning in the higher grades, but singing must always be in the center. In our musical elementary schools, instruments are not compulsory, but many children want to play an instrument, and follow the advice of their teachers in choosing a suitable one. In those schools, our purpose is not so much the training of instrumental soloists, as it is the preparation of students for participation in chamber and orchestral music. Some of the larger schools are able to perform concerti of Vivaldi or other works of similar difficulty. The nonplaying pupils are the performing students' understanding and thankful audience, and once grown up, they will be the best audience for great music. In this way they fulfill the purpose of those schools and of all our endeavors.

The pedagogical approach used by Leonard Bernstein in his television programs, also published in book form with records, is most interesting and witty, but is by no means a satisfying way to educate a truly expert public. This is a most crucial problem, and in every country one can notice the disproportion between the performing artist and his audience. Though attempts to educate a music-loving and musically knowledgeable public are numerous, their success is dependent upon developing an audience of active listeners.

This is the goal to be reached in our schools, but music educators give their pupils much more. As they make students better musicians, they also make them better human beings. There is a German saying that a bad musician may be a fairly good man, but a good musician is, *ceteris paribus*, a better man. The good musician certainly is more balanced, manysided, and equally developed bodily and mentally. The introduction of a music program that perpetuates tradition and provides a solid musical foundation into the curriculum of general education would greatly enrich the human race.

The author was Project Director of a federally-financed Kodaly Fellowship Program in which ten young American musicians went to Hungary in 1968, after a summer of intense language training, to observe the Hungarian national effort to improve musical literacy through the Kodaly teaching plan. The next year, following the summer in which they prepared materials for use in the United States, the ten Kodaly fellows worked in three American school districts with daily classes of musically gifted children who volunteered for the program. The New Haven model for Kodaly instruction is one of the results of this work. This article, reprinted from the Fall 1971 issue of *College Music Symposium*, Journal of the College Music Society, was delivered as an address at the Seattle meeting of the Society for Ethnomusicology.

# KODALY AND EDUCATION: A MUSICOLOGICAL NOTE

Alexander L. Ringer

The notion of universal musical literacy is as old as the idea of basic education for all. Both the Protestant Reformation and the French Revolution were milestones in its history. As modern life developed, however, specific knowledge and understanding of music rarely went far beyond the narrow circles of polite society. The late Zoltan Kodaly, himself a conservatory-trained product of that society as it existed in late 19th century Europe, awakened rather early to the realization that musical literacy, potentially a highly effective agent of socialization, operated primarily as an attribute of status and hence, by implication, of discrimination. So conceived it retained but a fraction of its vast potential, as far as he was concerned. But, as a means of leading urbanized man back to his historical roots, as an effective channel of communication between people of every possible cultural level and orientation, above all as a key to a country's hidden cultural strength, it seemed to him, the conscious and systematic pursuit of musical skills amounted to nothing less than a national imperative.

When Kodaly and his friend Bartok decided to share both the musical and the material lives of the Hungarian peasants, they did so precisely because they wished to probe the very roots of an artistic vitality that had managed to survive countless invasions, occupations, and other assorted national disasters. They soon discovered not only that broad segments of Hungary's non-literate population were totally and actively immersed in their traditional music, but also that the remarkable flexibility and expressive wealth of this music was due, at least in part, to the very absence of *a priori* limitations of the kind imposed upon literate musical cultures by the inherent rigidity of notational conventions. As a result, Kodaly based his subsequent didactic work toward the establishment of an organically conceived national program of musical education on two non-negotiable principles: (1) only singing furnishes an acceptable common denominator for all children irrespective of socio-economic background, and (2) singing and hearing must precede notation, lest music reading and writing be reduced to the level of largely meaningless cerebral exercises.

Kodaly's determination never to impinge upon these two closely related principles implies, for one, that the current tendency in educationist circles to associate his name with that of Carl Orff rests on an unfortunate misunderstanding. For Orff, catering to the sophisticated musical culture of his native Germany, has always promoted instrumental skills, not to speak of the fact that his rhythmic "system" gives priority to metrical patterns, whereas Kodaly thought of meter essentially as a subcategory of rhythm limited in both historical and ethnic scope. Moreover, totally inspired as they are, by the vocal folk music of the Hungarian countryside, many of Kodaly's didactic compositions have unique language-determined characteristics that render them fundamentally unsuitable for translation and for adaptation. As Berlioz put it upon his return from Hungary well over a century ago, Hungarian is a very beautiful language, provided one knows how to speak it.

Kodaly's conviction that children will learn how to read

and write music with lasting success only when allowed to make direct connections with aurally familiar materials went counter to some cherished assumptions of the genteel tradition. Though certainly influenced by his intimate contacts with orally transmitted musical cultures, this particular doctrine was no doubt socially motivated by Kodaly's profound distaste for any elitist form of education that permitted specially favored individuals to reach unusually high degrees of creative and recreative sophistication while excluding, by its very nature the vast majority of the people.

Whatever the case, in purely musical terms his study of oral tradition not only revealed the vast artistic possibilities of a limited repertory of musical formulae continuously modified, rearranged, and fused in a variety of ways, it also suggested that the repeated use of such pre-existing patterns might well be what makes improvisation possible, indeed typical of a great deal of folk music. He may or may not have subscribed to the psychoanthropological view which holds that every child goes through a condensed version of the historical evolution of his species; his approach to musical education certainly suggests that he tended to identify the creative potential of children with that of pre-literate rather than literate man. At any rate, the official Hungarian curriculum inspired by him more or less follows conceptual changes in Western music from the improvisational and pseudo-improvisational patterns of the largely pre-literate Middle Ages to the highly sophisticated cerebral manipulations of the Schoenberg school. Thus, second graders are asked to develop their rhythmic and melodic vocabulary first by replying motivically to a musical "question," then by creating their own motivic combinations and re-combinations without guidance of any sort. And while these children, like their adult counterparts in so-called primitive societies, will make the most of a familiar idiom, they develop faculties of speech with amazing promptness and spontaneity.

Kodaly, a contemporary of Koffka, Kohler, and other pioneers in the field of *Gestalt* psychology, was concerned not so much with scales, modes, or other artificial patterns of pitch selection, as with motivic pitch groupings capable of repetition, transposition, inversion, and rotation. Even though his overriding concern with pentatonic melodies was undoubtedly a direct outgrowth of his ethnomusicological research, one wonders whether it was not Kodaly, the composer, who cherished the inherent motivic structure of pentatonicism. After all, leaving aside the fact that the major scale consists of two identical disjunct tetrachords, heptatonic scales, as employed in Western music, are on the whole motivically neutral, whereas pentatonic patterns are by definition motivically determined. Associated with oral traditions lacking in theoretical frames of reference, they neglect scalar considerations in the interest of maximal utilization of minimal pitch materials. Thus, the pattern D, F, G, A, C, consists of a basic motif (minor third plus major second) and its retrograde inversion, pivoting on G. And judicious manipulation of this motivic substance can produce any number of different yet intimately related tunes.

Taking his cues from the naturally descending tendency of Hungarian folksongs as well as children's games overheard at home and elsewhere, Kodaly recognized the descending minor third sol-mi as a virtually universal motivic nucleus easily expanded through addition of upper and/or lower neighboring tones (la, re). Moreover, he correctly observed that children are capable of perceiving implicit relationships at an early educational stage and, without necessarily being able to make the appropriate cerebral judgments, manage to assimilate the crucial point that something big can grow out of something small, depending on how one deals with its constituent elements. For all we know, the mental processes involved are akin to those activated by play with interchangeable building units. Like the building block unit, the musical motif can be turned upside down for purposes other than those it served in its original form and can be pointed sidewise, as it were. Hence, the motivic approach promotes a relatively effortless realization that unity and diversity far from being incompatible are actually inseparable aspects of any organically conceived structure. Kodaly, deeply concerned with social values, could not but make the most of this general lesson to be derived from the conceptual study of music.

In the American context, this fascination with pure melodic-rhythmic forces assumes very special significance. Indoctrinated with the "familiar" style, American music educators take the primacy of functional harmony virtually for granted. Their "accompanying" instrument is usually the pianoforte, the most harmonically oriented of all Western instruments. And more often than not the piano does not serve to accompany but, more accurately, to guide. At any rate, American children are exposed from an early age to triads and their simplest combinations, as well as the tempered tuning of the modern keyboard. Kodaly, to be sure, emphasized the vocal element for a great variety of reasons. One of these was no doubt the lack of instruments, especially pianos, in rural Hungarian schools. An equalitarian at heart, he naturally looked for ways and means of promoting music in all the schools in a manner that would minimize material disadvantages. But in the end he was first and foremost a musician, not a sociologist, let alone a politician, indeed more of a humanist than an equalitarian, who realized that harmony in the Western functional sense does not come "naturally" to human beings but is a contrivance of civilization. This is not to say that he personally disdained harmony. On the contrary, unlike Bartok's, his own work as a composer falls plainly into the final stages of functional harmony. But he was not unaware of the tenuously temporary nature of the various last-minute efforts to salvage a tradition that had dominated two full centuries of European art music. Clearly, Debussy's modal and whole-tone experiments represented no less an attempt to re-establish the primacy of melodic continuity than Schoenberg's early "a-tonality." In either case an historically conscious composer was trying to avoid the melodic-rhythmic stagnation produced by the over-extension of functional harmony. This is clearly not the place to enter into an analysis of early twentieth century European music at the cross roads. But it is worth recalling in the present context that those who were to determine the principal currents of twentieth century music in nearly every instance reiterated melodic-rhythmic elements at the expense of the harmonic component.

The ultimate value of a Kodaly-inspired program, then, lies in its relevance to both twentieth century music, as practiced in sophisticated Western circles, and a wide range of the world's cultures. In other words, whereas the teaching of music in American schools deals restrictively with an exceedingly limited repertory, the Kodaly approach centers on fundamental musical issues manifested in many musics in a variety of ways depending on specific socio-historical conditions. If Kodaly decided to draw primarily upon the musical heritage of his native country, he did so not merely for ethnocentric reasons but also because that particular heritage was apt to demonstrate a number of such issues concretely and at a high aesthetic level. By the same token, he never understood why non-Hungarians would want to take over lock, stock, and barrel, either his materials or a general methodology evolved in response to a particular national need. Conscious perhaps more than anyone else, except for Bartok, of the unique fusion of linguistic and musical elements in the folk songs of Hungary, he could hardly condone their indiscriminate use in translations that often served to distort the musical effect without enhancing textual comprehension.

Any attempt to match in the American classroom, even remotely, what is being accomplished daily in Hungarian schools will have to be based on indigenous American materials judiciously chosen, as Kodaly insisted, in accordance with specific didactic aims. A rather striking example may serve to illustrate this crucial point. One of the teachers engaged in an experiment in Kodaly-inspired teaching at an inner-city school in New Haven, Connecticut found it exceedingly difficult at first to activate the black children's seemingly limitless musical potential. But her problems were solved, at least to a point, once she tried singsong type melodies employing the lower pentatone sol, la, do, re, mi, instead of do, re, mi, sol, la, which characterizes so many tunes of Anglo-Saxon origin. "Needless to say," she wrote subsequently, "my inability to research the vast field of black music in depth probably forced me to ignore many other musical characteristics which would have made the music and its understanding more meaningful to the students."

When all is said and done, therefore, the fortunes of the Kodaly approach on the American educational scene will depend to a large extent upon the willingness of musicologists not only to do much needed field work in urban areas but also to analyze and subsequently prepare materials specifically for the educational advancement of children hailing from those same areas. In order to give young blacks, Mexican-Americans, Puerto Ricans, or, for that matter, American Indians a truly meaningful musical education the schools will have to apply didactic insights gained from the study of their indigenous musical backgrounds and, more generally, cultural environments. What greater challenge could budding musicologists in search of immediate "relevance" conceive of than the creation of a new type of "applied" musicology designed to maximize the vast as yet untapped educational potential of the stylistic resources embedded in the totality, rather than a mere segment of America's many-splendored musical resources.

Carl Orff delivered this paper in a speech at the opening session of an Orff elementary education course at the University of Toronto in the summer of 1962. It was given in German and translated by Arnold Walter of the Faculty of Music of the University. The paper first appeared in the *Canadian Music Educator* and is reprinted here from the April-May 1963 issue of *Music Educators Journal.*

# THE SCHULWERK— ITS ORIGINS AND AIMS

Carl Orff
Translated by Arnold Walter

The nature of the Schulwerk, its aim and purpose, can perhaps best be explained by describing how it came into being. Looking back, I am tempted to call it a wild flower (being a passionate gardener I am given to such comparisons). Just as wild flowers grow wherever they find suitable conditions, so the Schulwerk grew and developed, finding nourishment in my work. It was not the result of a preconceived plan—I never would have been able to plan so far ahead—it simply arose from a need which I recognized. We all know from experience that wild flowers thrive in abundance while carefully tended garden flowers disappoint us sometimes; they lack the strength of natural growth.

Such natural growth has advantages and disadvantages. Those who look for a method or a ready-made system are rather uncomfortable with the Schulwerk; people with artistic temperament and a flair for improvisation are fascinated by it. They are stimulated by the possibilities inherent in a work which is never quite finished, in flux, constantly developing. It is only natural that such a procedure may be dangerous at times; it may run in the wrong direction. Anyone who wishes to advance on his own, needs a thorough professional training and, in addition, an intimate knowledge of the style of the Schulwerk, a grasp of its aim and potential.

Unfortunately, it has often been misinterpreted, exploited,

and falsified to the point of caricature. Yet a great amount of material sent to me year after year by truly outstanding teachers—letters, photographs, tapes, articles, reports—has confirmed and endorsed the soundness of my approach. I appreciate their attitude.

To return to its origins: in the 20's the younger generation was captivated by a new feeling for the body, for sport, gymnastics, and dance. Jaques-Dalcroze had helped to prepare the ground for the new movement; his "Institute for Music and Rhythm" in Hellerau became widely known. Rudolf Von Laban and Mary Wigman (to mention only those two) were at the height of their careers. Laban was a magnificent teacher, an outstanding choreographer; his book on the dance earned him great fame. Mary Wigman—a disciple of Dalcroze and Laban and a great star in her own right—created a new expressive dance. The impact of their work was enormous; both teaching and performing were deeply influenced by it. It was a time when numerous schools for gymnastics and dance came into being. Being keenly interested in the whole movement, I added to their number. Together with Dorothea Guenther— she was to become one of the outstanding teachers in her field—I established, in 1924, the Guenther Schule in Munich. Uppermost in my mind was the creation of a rhythmic education; also the realization of my main idea that music and movement ought to be taught simultaneously, supplementing one another and intimately connected. How necessary this was I had learned in the theatre. Working with singers, actors, dancers, and musicians, I discovered a surprising lack of rhythmic awareness, a total absence of proper training.

The most remarkable thing about the Guenther Schule was probably the fact that one of its founders and directors happened to be a musician. Musical activities were looked upon with favor; I had every opportunity to try out my ideas, to experiment. There was no doubt in my mind that the training had to be totally different from what was customary at that time. The accent was on rhythm. We had to find instruments that lent themselves to this approach. It was my ambition to bring all students to the point where they could accompany their own dances and exercises as competently as musicians would. I did not want to have anything to do with piano accompaniments which were then (and still are) being used in the training of movement. I wanted the students to become musicians in their own right. Wigman's experiments showed me the way; I still remember every detail of her sensational witchdance, accompanied only by African rattles. Instead of making them play the piano (so out of place in a school of movement and dance) I taught the students instruments that had rhythmical impact, primitive appeal—and were easy to handle. Of course such instruments have first to be found. There was no shortage of percussion straight and simple, whether native or exotic; the current development of jazz had seen to that: we had only to choose what we wanted. An independent ensemble, however, called for melody and bordun instruments. For that reason we proceeded to build rhythm instruments capable of carrying melody—xylophones, metallophones, and glockenspiels in various sizes and forms. Some were new, some influenced by medieval and exotic models. The trogxylophones for instance, had little in common with the xylophones usually found in orchestras; it was actually a descendant of highly developed Indonesian types. In Karl Maendler, a piano and harpsichord manufacturer of genius, I found a man who was sympathetic to my ideas and willing to experiment. It took him years to develop all those instruments which are taken for granted today; but he succeeded in adding incomparable, irreplaceable timbres to our ensemble. New also were the ranges—there appeared soprano, alto, tenor, and bass models of both xylophones and metallophones. New was a playing technique made possible by the addition of resonance boxes and by the use of soft mallets; the sound became infinitely more variable.

If I may digress for a moment, I would like to mention that these perfected xylophones and metallophones have found their way into our opera and symphony orchestras. I myself use them in quantity in *Antigone* and *Oedipus* (ten to twelve large xylophones) where they dominate the orchestral timbre.

But back to the Guenther Schule; the flute soon joined the

ensemble as a melody instrument. It is, of course, one of the oldest, one might say a primeval instrument. After experimenting with exotic varieties I decided to use the recorder. Together with harpsichords and gambas it had been rediscovered in the course of the revival of old music. Until then, that is until the first years of our century, recorders had been hidden away in museums. With the help of Curt Sachs, at that time curator of the famous Berlin collection of ancient instruments, I was able to assemble a quartet of recorders built after old models—descant, treble, tenor and bass. How the interest in recorders had suddenly developed can be gleaned from the fact that Fritz Joede started to use them at about the same time in his work with the Youth Movement; but only for the performance of old music.

I still remember the day when we received the very first quartet of recorders in the Guenther Schule—I remember our helplessness and confusion; there wasn't anybody who could tell us how to play them. We had to work it out by trial and error, and did so in a completely unhistorical manner. I have always regretted that recorder playing (particularly as practiced in the Youth Movement) became almost a pest, that the instruments fell so soon into ill repute. Mass production of cheap and unreliable models had a great deal to do with it; also the strange belief that anything and everything could be played on them.

For the bass part of our ensemble—sustained fifths and borduns—we used kettledrums, low xylophones, also strings: cellos, fiddles and gambas of all sorts. A group of plucked instruments consisting of lutes and guitars completed our ensemble.

Now music had to be created, composed, or arranged from satisfactory original source material; folk music (both native and foreign) proved very valuable in this respect. In my teaching I tried to bring the students to the point where they could invent music of their own to accompany movement, however modest such inventions might be at first. They grew out of spontaneous improvisations in which a student could freely express himself. Our pieces were not first written out and afterwards performed. They were extemporizations. After much playing some might be set in notation. Reading was rather uncommon; the music was learned by heart and played from memory. At the end we did, of course, write down what we played in order not to forget it, in order also to illustrate our pedagogical intentions. Thus originated the first edition of the Schulwerk in 1930. Its first volume began with the statement: "The Schulwerk concerns itself with the primary forces and forms of music." In quick succession there appeared additional volumes such as "Playing Percussion and Tambourine," "Playing Kettledrums," "Playing Xylophones," "Playing Recorders," also "Dances and Instrumental Pieces for Various Combinations."

Gunild Keetman, my erstwhile pupil and lifelong assistant, collaborated with me on the development of the instrumental ensemble and on the preparation of the volumes just mentioned. Hans Bergese and Wilhelm Twittenhoff also assisted me in various ways. In due course the Guenther school boasted an ensemble of dancers with an orchestra of their own. Music and choreography were supervised by Gunild Keetman and Maja Lex, respectively. Dancers and players were interchangeable; it also happened that suitable instruments (flutes, cymbals, drums, etc.) were integrated in the dance itself. To illustrate the diversity and variety of such an orchestra let me list the instruments employed: Recorders, xylophones, the metallophones of all ranges, glockenspiels, kettledrums, small drums, tomtoms, gongs, various kinds of cymbals, triangles, tune bells; sometimes also fiddles, gambas, spinettinos, and portatives. The group toured Germany and other European countries; its performances were invariably successful. In addition the ensemble appeared at teachers' conventions and educational conferences, thereby drawing attention to the Schulwerk.

Music educators had taken an interest in my experiments from the beginning. Foremost among them was Leo Kestenberg, most influential at that time because of his position in the Ministry of Education in Berlin. Assisted by Dr. Preussner and Dr. Walter, he espoused the cause of the Schulwerk;

in fact he planned to test it on a grand scale in the public schools—a decision that led to immediate publication of the Schulwerk material. I still admire the courage of my publisher friends Ludwig and Willy Strecker (owners of Schott in Mainz) in printing it—and that at a time when the instruments called for were still in scant supply. Kestenberg's plan, however, was never put into operation. He soon had to relinquish his position, a political wave sweeping away all of the ideas which we had realized. Whatever was saved from the wreckage was misunderstood and misinterpreted.

During the war the Guenther Schule was completely destroyed, the buildings gutted by fire, the instruments lost. It was never rebuilt. Times had changed; I had given up teaching. And yet I expected, subconsciously, a new call.

The call came. It came in 1948. It was quite literally a call—from the Bavarian radio. One of their officials, a Dr. Panofsky, had discovered an out-of-print recording from the time of the Guenther Schule and had played it to the director of school programming. The music on the record was scored for the ensemble I have described earlier. What they asked me was this: "Could you write us some music on these lines? Music that children might be able to play by themselves? We think that it would appeal to them. Three or four broadcasts perhaps?"

I was working on the score of *Antigone* at the time and was completely out of touch with educational problems; but I found the offer attractive, it presented a challenge. A challenge indeed! The instruments which had been used in the Guenther Schule were gone. Times were bad, raw material unavailable—how would we get new instruments? But that was not all. The old Schulwerk had addressed itself to an older age group, to prospective teachers of movement and dance. As it stood it was not applicable to children.

All of a sudden the tragic interruption of my earlier work became meaningful—I saw in a flash where rhythmical education really ought to begin: when a child enters school—or earlier still, at pre-school age. Although my previous experiments were out of date now because of my new insights, my years of experience had prepared me for a fresh start. That the unity of music and movement is still naturally present in the child (adolescents have already lost it, and must relearn it) is so sadly overlooked that it became the cornerstone of my new pedagogical work. I suddenly understood what the first Schulwerk had lacked: the singing voice, the word. A child quite naturally starts with a call, a rhyme, with text and tune together; movement, play and song coalesce and integrate. I would never have been able to bring myself to "write a few pieces for children" for radio, seeing how busy I was at that time; but I was fascinated by the idea of a musical education completely geared to the child. So I accepted the offer and went to work, but in my own way.

I began to see things in the right perspective. "Elemental" was the password, applicable to music itself, to the instruments, to forms of speech and movement. What does it mean? The Latin word *elementarius*, from which it is derived means "pertaining to the elements, primeval, basic". What, then, is elemental music? Never music alone, but music connected with movement, dance, and speech—not to be listened to, meaningful only in active participation. Elemental music is pre-intellectual, it lacks great form, it contents itself with simple sequential structures, ostinatos, and miniature rondos. It is earthy, natural, almost a physical activity. It can be learned and enjoyed by anyone. It is fitting for children.

Gunild Keetman and I, assisted by an experienced educator, shaped the first broadcasts and started to build the series. We worked with children and for children. The result was the new Schulwerk.

Our melodic starting point was the falling minor third. The compass was gradually widened until it reached a pentatonic scale without half tones. Linguistically we started with name calls, counting-out rhymes and the simplest of songs. Here was a world easily accessible to children. I wasn't thinking of especially gifted ones. What I had in mind was the education in the broadest terms, applicable to modestly gifted children and even those with very little talent. I knew from experience that few children are completely unmusical, that almost every child can comprehend and enjoy music. Incompetent teachers too often fail to recognize what is inherent in the child. Such teachers do a great deal of damage.

We began our broadcasts in the Autumn of 1948 with unprepared school children between the ages of eight and twelve using whatever was left of the Guenther Schule instruments. The children were fascinated. As they played, their enthusiasm made its mark on the listener. It soon became clear (as I had foreseen) that the short series of broadcasts originally planned was wholly inadequate; that we were at the beginning of a far-reaching development. Where it would lead was impossible to predict. The response from the schools was beyond all expectation. Children were excited, they all wanted to learn to play that kind of music; requests for information mounted, people wanted to know where instruments could be bought. A young pupil of old Maendler, Klauss Becker, came to our assistance. With whatever material he could lay hands on, he put together the first xylophones and metallophones for the new Schulwerk. He too was successful. After a year he was able to open a workshop of his own called Studio 49, where our instruments are steadily being improved.

Soon the radio organized competitions for the children who played, as well as for the children who were listening, with instruments as prizes. Rhymes and simple poems had to be set to music; the compositions (both melody and accompaniment) had to be written out. The results were most gratifying and proved to us that the broadcasts had been properly understood and digested.

They lasted five full years and laid the groundwork for five basic volumes which appeared between 1950 and 1954. Their title—*Music for Children.*

In 1949 Gunild Keetman joined the staff of the Mozarteum in Salzburg to give regular courses in the Schulwerk; Dr. Preussner, the Director of the Academy, had known it since his early days with Kestenberg. Here it was possible to pay more attention to movement, an aspect that naturally doesn't lend itself to broadcasting. Demonstrations and performances aroused interest. Delegates to international conferences held at the Mozarteum became acquainted with the Schulwerk and decided to make use of it in their own countries. One of them was Arnold Walter, who prevailed upon Doreen Hall to study with Keetman in Salzburg and to introduce the Schulwerk into Canada after her return. Daniel Hellden carried it to Sweden, Mina Lange to Denmark. It also found its way to Switzerland, Belgium, Holland, England, Portugal, Yugoslavia, Latin America, Turkey, Israel, Greece and finally Japan. The tapes of the original broadcasts did much to prepare the way. They were re-broadcast by many foreign stations.

All this made it necessary to translate and adapt the German edition. It wasn't simply a question of translation but rather of using a country's folklore, its nursery rhymes and children's songs in the same way as the German ones have been used in the original. Doreen Hall and Arnold Walter prepared the first foreign version; since then the Schulwerk has been published in Swedish, Flemish, Danish, English, French, Spanish, and Portuguese, with a Japanese edition in preparation.

After concluding the five volumes of *Music for Children*, two sets of recordings, and a film, I thought that I had come to the end of my pilgrimage. But the growing interest in the Schulwerk, the editing just mentioned, the additions of whole new fields,[1] such as music therapy, kept me extremely busy. They still do. Requests for teachers, the discovery also that the Schulwerk has all too often been wrongly interpreted convinced me of the need for an authentic training center. Once again it was Dr. Preussner who came to my assistance by creating such a center in the Mozarteum; in this he was generously supported by the Austrian authorities whose help I gratefully acknowledge. The new Institute devotes itself exclusively to the Schulwerk and, in particular, to the training of teachers. It attracts students from all over the world.

---

[1] A few months after Orff made his speech, a therapeutical and sociopedagogical research division was to have been added, with Wilhelm Keller in charge.

The author of this article was one of the translators of the English edition of Carl Orff's *Music for Children*. The article is reprinted from the January 1959 issue of *The Instrumentalist*.

# CARL ORFF'S MUSIC FOR CHILDREN

Arnold Walter

A quarter of a century ago I attended a recital given by students of a school of modern dance—a recital I have never forgotten; it is as clear in my memory as if it had happened yesterday. The place was Munich; the school called itself "Guntherschule;" movement and dance were strongly influenced by Mary Wigman, with an accent on improvisation, but what captivated me completely was the coordination of music and movement, the fact (unique in my experience) that the students were uncommonly well trained in both disciplines.

These students made their own music, now dancing, now playing with equal grace and competence; the whole performance looked and sounded as if it had been improvised on the spot. Dancers would stop dancing to take their place in the "orchestra;" musicians would leave their instruments to join the dancers singly or in groups; sound and motion seemed to be created by the same impulses. One couldn't help feeling that something was coming to life here which had long been forgotten in our civilization: the primeval power, the magic effect of music which "moves" us quite literally—which makes us move and dance as the Greeks did and as the Orient still does today. And one wished that all young musicians could have the privilege of such training, acquiring the rhythmical awareness and melodic imagination of those dancers improvising on flutes and drums.

For the "orchestra" wasn't the usual combination of strings, woodwinds and brasses; it consisted of recorders, viols, bells, glockenspiels, xylophones, and every known kind of drum; small portative organs were on one end of the scale, double-headed Indian drums on the other. The instruments on the stage looked like a page from a medieval manuscript. The music itself had an archaic flavor reminding one of trouveres, jongleurs, and Italian dances of the 14th century; but it had also a very modern one bringing Stravinsky to mind, particularly the Stravinsky of *Les Noces*. The reasons were obvious: rhythm was the predominating element; melody grew out of rhythm as it were; drones and ostinati formed the accompaniment; harmony, if used at all, restricted itself to parallel motion resulting in organum-like effects.

No doubt this was a very unusual kind of music. It had the appeal of primitive strength, and yet, it was curiously satisfying to modern ears; it didn't accompany the dance, it created it; and it seemed an ideal medium to teach young people what music was all about—to teach them how to respond to it wholly, with every muscle and nerve, with body and soul. The man responsible for the recital was Carl Orff, in those days the musical director of the Guntherschule. Today he is very famous; his operas and scenic oratorios are performed and recorded everywhere. It is sufficient to mention the *Carmina Burana, Der Mond* and *Antigone;* but however well known as a composer, he is equally famous as a music educator. He had the happy inspiration to teach children the same way he had taught these fascinating dancers, with quite astonishing results.

The pedagogical value of his approach was recognized at once. Radio Munich made use of it in countless broadcasts; and Schott in Mainz published a manual called *Music for Children (Das Schulwerk)* which is in the process of being translated into Turkish and Japanese (it is already available in many European languages); Orff's influence on modern music education is without parallel.

*Orff's Pedagogical Approach*

What made it so? Orff starts with the premise (learned from ethnomusicology) that the musical development of children roughly corresponds to the growth of music history; rhythm precedes (and is stronger than) melody; melody precedes (and is stronger than) harmony. If you take a child, if you sit him down at the piano, tell him where middle C is and proceed to teach him the *Minuet in G*, you introduce him to rhythm, melody, harmony and instrumental technique at one and the same time. He might survive it, certainly; but the chances are that he will learn the piece mechanically, without feeling for rhythm, without enthusiasm for the very polite (and most un-childlike) melody, without appreciation of functional harmony.

A teacher following Orff's precepts will do exactly the opposite. He will start with speech patterns, using single words, phrases or nursery rhymes to illustrate the various types of measure which are experienced rather than explained. Such rhythmical formulas are reproduced by stamping, clapping, and finally on instruments. That is all very primitive and elementary, but that is precisely what it ought to be: elementary, basic. A child finding it difficult to grasp a rhythmical pattern or to hold his own in a rhythmic canon has no business playing the *Minuet in G*.

*Melodic Materials*

Melody is made to grow out of rhythm—imperceptibly, slowly; it is treated with *infinite care*. Two notes are introduced at first, then three and four, finally five; there is great emphasis on pentatonic tunes, for a variety of reasons. They do not depend on accompaniment, they don't imply harmony, they are the best possible material for improvisation (the technique of Javanese gamelan orchestras proves the point). They are also very beautiful; does anyone know a really bad pentatonic tune?

Major and minor melodies are introduced in due course, but as a final stage in a carefully planned development. And it is precisely that development, the gradual widening-out of the tonal space in the child's mind which is the governing idea of the whole approach. Cadential harmony is treated in a similar way, not as a starting point but as a goal to be reached; familiar chord progressions are preceded by drones, ostinati, and parallel motion.

## Use of Instruments

Rhythm patterns, melodies, and ostinato figures are tried out and played on the instruments mentioned earlier. These instruments are anything but toys; they are carefully selected and contrasted, they are in fact replicas of medieval ensembles, as meaningful to children now as they were to grown-up people in those days. They are difficult enough to be a challenge to a child yet simple enough to make improvisation possible. And that is what Orff wants more than anything else—*to enable children to improvise, to invent their own rhythms, melodies, and accompanying figures.* It is a well-known fact that younger children appear often more gifted than older ones: their fertile curiosity, their spontaneous reactions have not been stifled yet by ready-made learning which psychologists recognize as a form of "adult pressure." Such pressure can be avoided only by making the greatest possible use of a child's creative ability. Beauty (says Jean Piaget) is of value only when recreated by those who discover it.

## A Truly Creative Approach

It seems that much of our teachings can be summed up in the phrase just quoted "ready-made learning." The child repeats what he has been taught without discovering music by recreating it. But it is not easy to avoid the traditional ways and means of teaching. It means avoiding all the systems, methods, and primers on the market; avoiding the usual fare of children's songs and easy pieces—avoiding even major modes and functional harmony, to start with at least. And it would be a mistake to think that Orff's book contains a ready-made system to be taught chapter by chapter; it is not that kind of book at all. It points in the right direction but the road to be traveled must be *discovered* by the teacher himself. Such a teacher must be capable of molding musical material without help from printed pages; he must deal with rhythm, melody, and harmony as painters deal with colors and sculptors with clay—he must be able to encourage children to play with sound objects, to form them, to "compose" them. Which pre-supposes of course that he can do all that himself.

Is that too much to be asked of a music teacher? Is there any reason why music teachers could not do what art teachers have done so successfully in recent years? Carl Orff certainly blazed a trail which will be followed by many. He realized that there is music in children; but he realized also that it is fundamentally different from the music they would want to learn later on—that it was necessary to breach the gap, not by ready-made learning but by traversing the various stages of music's own growth. That sounds simple. But all great discoveries have an air of simplicity—once they have been made.

This article deals with Dalcroze, Orff, and Kodaly concepts, and describes in detail one application of them in an American school. The article is reprinted from the January 1968 *Music Journal.*

# NEW DIMENSIONS IN MUSIC EDUCATION

Ruth G. Frost

Music education in the U.S. is catching up to the twentieth century! Today's pre-school and elementary level students are beginning to receive a musical education relevant to their daily life. Widespread recognition of the usefulness of music in developing a sense of rhythm and coordination in children has prompted educators to cease regarding the teaching of music as an end in itself. This changing concept is slowly bringing music into its rightful place as an integral part of the over-all learning experience of our young students.

This transformation has begun to have an effect upon the public schools of the nation (notably California and Illinois). although these concepts have been recognized and utilized in private elementary schools and music schools for some time.

Historically speaking, the musical metamorphosis in education began to develop at the turn of the century when the fresh ideas of Emile Jaques-Dalcroze began to filter across the sea from Switzerland. Developing what came to be known as the "Dalcroze Method of Eurythmics," this music professor linked music and body movements to music. He believed that this would facilitate a rapid communication between body and mind to make a feeling for rhythm a physical experience.

But it was not until almost half a century later, when Carl Orff, German music educator and composer, wrote music and devised instruments especially for the purpose of introducing young people to music that any fundamental change began to be felt on this side of the Atlantic. Using Dalcroze as his springboard, initially, Orff created music for the young dance students in his school. In 1948, he revised his earlier work and developed "Das Schulwerk" into an educational system specifically for music. In addition to the music, he designed a series of flexible percussion instruments. By 1954 his philosophy of teaching was embodied in his *Music for Children* and a distribution system for the instruments and printed materials was set up in this country.

Meanwhile in Hungary another prominent composer was busy creating his contribution to early musical education. Beginning with something very old to create something very new, Zoltan Kodaly coordinated the old solfege syllables with a series of new hand signals to aid the students in associating an incipient musical sound with a visual pattern. Kodaly's system, which aided the improvement of sight-singing facility, was introduced in this country several years after the Orff techniques were applied. A few alert music educators recognized that the incorporation of both the Orff and Kodaly concepts into the musical curriculum would inaugurate a new era in elementary music education.

One such veteran teacher is Gertrude Barlow who has been applying the Orff and Kodaly techniques in her classes at the Third Street Music School since 1962 (see *Music Journal,* February, 1962), and also at the Iona Grammar School in New Rochelle.

We contacted Mrs. Barlow to see if her opinion had changed over the years. "Yes," she still found the Orff and Kolady methods extremely effective teaching tools and was even more enthusiastic about them than when we interviewed her five years before. We made an appointment to find out why.

We discovered that Mrs. Barlow's enthusiasm about the new teaching techniques stems from their flexibility, which allows the teacher to adapt them to the needs and background of her pupils as well as the scope of her own imagination. Specifically, Orff has laid down the principles in his musical syllabus, encouraging teachers in each country to utilize and develop the musical characteristics of the native culture.

Among the innovations introduced by Mrs. Barlow since the inception of Orff at the Third Street Music School was the gradual lowering of the age of the student classes. Beginning in 1962 with seven year olds, Mrs. Barlow has now organized groups down to the four-year age level. Drawing upon the insight she has gained from her five consecutive years of work with the new teaching methods, she asserted that her gradually acquired perspective has enabled her to judge the effect of the earlier Orff music training on her older students.

Comparing six year olds who have had the earlier training with those who did not, Mrs. Barlow finds her efforts in initiating instruction at an earlier age justified. In almost every case, those students who had the early training were able to absorb it and were more advanced musically than those of their age group who had no exposure to this type of learning experience.

In discussing the content of her year's work with the four year olds, Mrs. Barlow pointed out that she limited class size to eight in this age range. She cautioned against too much verbalizing with this group and explained that she communicated with the tone of her voice, expression in her eyes and body movement. Since the attention span at this age is short, this teacher believes that eight-bar songs should be the maximum length. Students make music and participate from the very first class in singing rhythmic speech exercises (done with riddles and proverbs) and walking and clapping to rhythmic patterns.

Specifically the songs concentrate on a melodic line, and Mrs. Barlow's goal is to create a "group awareness as well as discipline in listening." Simultaneously, diction development combined with rhythmic clapping is introduced. This, if all goes smoothly, is eventually transferred to the percussion instruments. A typical specific exercise:

"Juba this, and Juba that,
Juba caught a yellow cat.
Juba up and Juba down,
Juba jumping up and down."

Since physical movement is important in this age range,

Mrs. Barlow has developed a series of walking, skipping and running steps that are related to the rhythms she wishes the children to learn. Other participating exercises utilized are game songs about the zoo, seesaw or similar topics related to that of the specific age group. The question-and-answer method in rhythm and melody is also used to stimulate the imagination in a controlled area.

The rewards of working with the four year olds are reaped when they become five and you can measure their achievements against the five year olds who have not had early instruction, Mrs. Barlow pointed out. The musically "educated" five year old can recognize meter, walk to note values and participate in playing with the musical flash cards that are used for rhythmic and melodic devices. Also, they are ready to improvise on their percussion instruments, transferring the rhythms on the cards to these instruments, with one pupil holding a whole note or "four count" note and another playing some half notes or "two count" notes.

More speech patterns, which Mrs. Barlow characterized as "pure Orff," are developed contrapuntally. She cited the following as an example:

> "Johnny lost his coat,
> Johnny lost his hat.
> Johnny lost his scarf,
> What do you think of that?"

For this one, the class is divided into two groups, with the second group entering on cue to form counterpoint.

Melody is stressed in this age group as well as rhythm, and some thirty songs are introduced during the school year. There is some unison singing as well as two-part work. As an accompaniment, a simple two-tone ostinato is introduced initially, and creates what Orff labeled "a carpet of sound." Often this experience prompts the children to improvise on their own, as they seek to express themselves musically at home on whatever instrument is available. The young students are inclined to create more interesting and complex patterns when working independently.

This is the time Mrs. Barlow applies Kodaly's techniques to ear training instruction. She introduces the Kodaly hand signals to the *sol-mi* syllables applying them to the first calls of the child, such as "mommy" or "daddy," in minor thirds and then adds word combinations, such as "rain, rain go away," that lend themselves to this method. The children sing back the syllables.

For the five year olds that have not had previous musical training, Mrs. Barlow stresses the rhythmic area, working with the children until they distinguish between whole, half and quarter notes. Ear training and singing techniques stress raising the pitch, and when an instrument is introduced it is usually a xylophone that has had all but two of the bars removed. The two notes left on the instrument are coordinated with calls and other combinations in minor thirds that the children had been singing. This is the beginning of intervallic listening.

Moving up to the six year olds who come without early training, Mrs. Barlow employs more complicated combinations since this group has more disciplined powers of concentration. Songs are more complicated, and speech patterns are orchestrated with percussion instruments. One favorite, Mrs. Barlow recited was the following:

"Railroad crossing—look out for the cars.
Can you spell that without any R's?"

This is done in four meter and three meter and is orchestrated in two parts.

Another variation of this activity is the singing of the "silent phrase" in which the students pulse the rhythm in the air and think the words. This technique teaches them to listen to the tune as well as to each other.

For the six year olds who have had musical training the previous year, it is time to start learning the techniques of blowing the tonette, and then on to the recorder. Mrs. Barlow teaches her group to hold the tonette correctly as well as the proper position of the mouth to prevent "overblowing," as well as to aid the student to develop respect for his instrument. In addition to the recorder, Orff instruments such as the soprano and alto glockenspiel, the soprano, alto and bass xylophone and the soprano and alto metallophone are introduced. After the group is familiar with the instruments, ensemble playing is introduced.

In the older groups (seven and eight year olds), Mrs. Barlow uses similar instruction as with the sixes. However, since the rate of learning is faster, they are able to understand and absorb more complex material. Theory is introduced and junior orchestras are formed. By now the child is at home in his musical environment and he can "play a piece of music without being chained to the notes as if he were reading a book."

Children fortunate enough to have this kind of musical training have received a permanent gift that will enrich their lives. If they continue to study a musical instrument they can move ahead to master its techniques while enjoying the music, having been freed of concern about the rhythms and other factors applicable to any instrument. This is completely opposite to the old concept of first stressing the technique of an instrument rather than the elements of the music itself.

Another surprising result of this type of educational experience, Mrs. Barlow noted, was that the introduction of a disciplined approach in a musical situation seems to aid in the improvement of conduct and attitudes of responsibility in other areas.

Even if they never develop proficiency upon a musical instrument, this kind of early training prepares them to be better listeners, creating more insight into what they hear, and thereby broadening their musical life. If properly taught, Mrs. Barlow summarized, this kind of learning experience becomes part of the child, conditioning him to listen properly so that he will be prepared to understand and enjoy every musical message throughout his life.

The author has successfully adapted and combined the Orff and Kodaly concepts in her workshops and written materials. Her article
appeared first in the April-May 1970 issue of *Musart.*

# MEDIA FOR HUMAN DEVELOPMENT

Grace C. Nash

Education is faced with a primary task of restoring a sense
of well-being to children—in a music centered, play media
classroom. According to the nature of childhood, his inborn
behavioral needs, music offers the most complete healing ingredients known to the Behavioral Sciences, but it must be
utilized to its fullest potential and with its most joyous appeal
for children.

In play where children are free from fear, where they are
using their subconscious minds in doing two, three and even
four things simultaneously, they are repeating patterns in
movement, speech and/or song—and the energizing force,
the organizer of these patterns is *rhythm.*

Rhythm may be considered the root of play. Acknowledged
that children learn the fastest in play, why not apply these
same techniques to learning and to human development? It
can be done through the ingredients of music and more con-
vincingly than through any other media. Orff and Kodaly
have shown the way; Dalcroze and Laban, too, and the work
of all of these men has been validated by the American Research Team of the Pillsbury Foundation Studies.[1]

Music is a natural medium for human development if it is
presented in the exciting, fresh approaches which have been
developed by Carl Orff, Zoltan Kodaly, Laban, Dalcroze and
others.

Why are the Orff-Schulwerk and the Kodaly systems of
music education so much discussed and so successful with
children? Because each approach begins with the basic nature
of childhood and utilizes the ingredients of music for the
child's personal development. Now if each approach is suc-

cessful on its own merits, imagine how splendid and more far reaching they become when combined (a reinforcement, a complement, an enrichment, each to the other). Then, adding Laban's Theory of Motion in exploration of Space, Time and Weight, as developed in England by Ann Driver, Rachel Percival and Vera Gray (with the acknowledged source of these principles coming from Dalcroze), imagine the strength of such a program for human development of children in American education. Exciting?—An understatement.

Placed in the center of the curriculum, this program could help children express their verbal experiences in sound, movement, color, (non-verbal media) and similarly non-verbal experiences can be translated into articulate and beautiful language. The five senses, movement, color and feeling would be combined with language and sound. Every child would be shown how to sing and control pitch knowledgeably. Their songs, poetry and dances would be self-accompanied on precision-tuned easy to play instruments (classroom instruments), an ensemble of beauty and excellence of esthetic proportions—student inspired and achieved.

Yes, in America we need both Orff and Kodaly, and Laban as well—not only to educate our children, but first to restore our five year olds to mental health, then to help them build toward sensitive, complete adults, even musically literate ones. How are we going to counteract existing hostile and dehumanizing environment? How are we going to develop their sensitivity, their hearing and awareness, their consideration and respect for their fellow man and property; these human qualities which have been allowed to deteriorate, and become numbed and dulled under present conditions? How are we going to restore and stimulate their natural creativity and imagination that has been lost for lack of understanding guidance, knowledge of and experience with nursery rhymes, nature (birds, trees, grass and streams) and play (exercise and fantasy)?

An ever increasing number of five year old children, having been exposed to three thousand hours of T.V. before entering school, are now hypertense and frustrated, deprived individuals! Visualize the child spending the equivalent of 260 days in front of T.V., when his real need is the outdoors, exercise and play which are as important to his growth and well-being as food. Looking at the content of T.V., what do deodorants, sex, violence in sordid detail, hard sell and double standards have to do with a child's world and his needs? As a result, many of our six year olds are now on tranquilizers, and in the affluent society, psychiatry is having to begin at four instead of forty-four!

Education has not caused this; environment has; but education must correct it, somehow. Two statements are quite indicative of the direction that visionary education will take, and is already taking:

1. To behold the greatest contemporary artist at work, simply observe an uninhibited child at play.

2. In the classroom of the future, work and play will be indistinguishable one from the other (in the learning process).

To know how to teach children then, we must first study and understand the nature of child. To know what to teach children we must find out what are their basic needs and future needs.

Movement, rhythm, song and repetition; these characteristics of play are also among child's basic needs, especially repetition, which is his security (for adults this is certainty).

Child's nature is imitative, imaginative, investigative and joyous, in a one to one, and eye to eye relationship. His five senses report to the brain; the sense of hearing (sound and rhythm) brings the first natural responses of movement, from birth onwards.

Rhythm and melody are present in the newborn infant and therefore should be utilized and sophisticated during his early growth period if he is to become a complete and whole person! These are the elements of music that hold tremendous potential for education in humanizing and accelerating the thought processes, sensitivity, corrective or remedial training and of course for well being. What adult who is clumsy, ever has a complete sense of well being? He is inhibited in practically every direction; yet, his basic right is to be free to move, to express and to communicate with any and all of his faculties of expression. Through education he should become an articulate individual—a music centered education.

Another important fact is that the harmonic chord and the repeated uninflected vertical beat do not lend themselves to human development;[2] yet the horizontal flow of melody and rhythm, phrased in language, in rhythmic line and movement, if utilized from the first with children, enables them to be free and articulate in growth to adulthood; they are not inhibited by a feeling of clumsiness or inability to respond.

Although little has been written about the potential factor of the subconscious mind and its deliberate application to a learning situation, it is present and in use in both Orff's and Kodaly's procedures through the ostinato or repeating pattern, similar to play. The subconscious or slave mind is the area of the brain which carries out orders given by the conscious mind. It is the non-thinking repeating part of the brain which also holds on to the child's self image of success or failure in his endeavors. In play, the subconscious keeps one, two or even three patterns going while the conscious mind listens and observes with utmost pleasure. Why not activate both areas of the child's brain, extending his conscious mind into performance also, and open up a greater potential and fuller use of the brain in early years? (Maximum use of the brain at present is estimated at 10% of the total brain potential.) Orff and Kodaly do just this enactment through use of rhythmic ostinato which can be taken over by the subconscious mind against the longer life of song or speech carried on by the conscious mind.

One of the earliest techniques of composition, the ostinato is recognized as one of the finest disciplinary techniques, not in or by itself, but in conjunction with other parts, one of which is the solo line. From self accompanied play into self accompanied music making, dance and poetry, singing the rhyme or prose text while playing, moving or clapping a rhythmic pattern, activates both areas of the brain, intensifies hearing while doing, and yet is so completely appealing that it is joyous and satisfying to the participant.

From one ostinato to several or many ostinati, with contrasting rhythmic, melodic, pitch level and timbre content makes for a thoroughly exciting ensemble as it builds with the lovely toned instruments of the Orff-Schulwerk assortments. This is, in itself, sensitivity training and should be a cumulative experience for every child through elementary years.

What of his singing voice? By nature the infant would sing before he speaks—but because few mothers sing to their babies, this natural response is left dormant and the child feels awkward or clumsy if he is asked to sing; although the mother tongue is assimilated by the age of three, the child knows not of his singing voice, neither can he see it, touch it, hold it or kick it. If he sings, he does so by an attempt at imitation and approximation of what he hears. Generally speaking the result is usually unsuccessful and out of tune.

Responsibility, in part, for this bad result in early school singing may be attributed to the wide range and inappropriate selection of children's songs in today's texts. If the voice is a fine musical instrument, and it most certainly is, then it merits respect and care in its development. Again, the nature of the instrument and the child are primary considerations. The universal chant or folk song of childhood,

So,  mi  la  so,  mi,

is the starting point.

These three tones provide the song media for children's nursery rhymes, nonsense verses, even fairly tales and their own experience songs, until the voice becomes entirely secure and accurate from any starting pitch and in any sequence of these three tones.

Now, through the work of Kodaly, the young child can see, feel and knowledgeably control his voice. Combining the hand signals (for tone syllables) with the movable "do," Kodaly has brought both the elements of play and the very concrete symbols of tone placement and tone relationship into singing growth—a challenging game that produces singing skills.

Human growth and sensitivity are extended and expanded with body movement, with Orff-like classroom instruments and with notation reading. Music becomes a many-splendored medium for human development only through one's own understanding and use of its potentials in the classroom. Peculiar though to all of the philosophies mentioned is the old Chinese proverb that states: "He who hears, forgets; he who sees, remembers; but he who does, knows."

---

[1] Santa Barbara, California (approximate dates, 1935-41) (out of print).

[2] All learning is horizontal or lateral. (Further explained in "Teacher's Manual," 1969 Edition by Grace C. Nash.)

Body movement is an important aspect of the music teaching methods presented in this book, and American music teachers and elementary classroom teachers show growing interest in it. This article, prepared especially for this book, presents a plan for teaching recorded music through dance.

# REALIZATION IN MOVEMENT AS A WAY OF COMPREHENDING MUSIC

Beth Landis

Having been interested in Dalcroze Eurhythmics from the beginning of my career, I have made use of movement with students from kindergarten through high school. Through application in the classroom of various principles of movement, along with continuous experimentation, I developed a somewhat different plan of working. The technique, a composite of my earlier experiences and an extension of them, became one of the most valuable and satisfying tools of my teaching career. It consists of realization of music in movement simultaneously with analytical listening. The music is a varied repertoire of compositions played on recordings. The purposes and benefits of the listening-movement experience are both musical and human.

Young children listen to "Polka" from the *Age of Gold* ballet by Shostakovich, and as dancing "skeletons" and "ghosts," they experience the rhythm, timbre, form, and other elements of the composition. Third graders leap, swirl, prance, and juggle, through their own carefully designed circus acts to "Dance of the Comedians" from *The Bartered Bride* by Smetana. Fifth-grade boys become "Napoleon's men" and "Hary Janos' men" as they dramatize in full detail "Battle and Defeat of Napoleon" from Kodaly's *Hary Janos Suite*. While listening and working out the dramatization, they give intense attention to details in the music. In many purposeful hearings they memorize it accurately, and throughout their lives in concert listening they will recall and antici-

pate sounds of the subtle as well as the obvious musical content. A class of ten-year-old children dance out all that they
hear in the Third Movement of Haydn's *Symphony No. 94*:
question and answer phrases, melodic patterns and their
variations, themes, instrumentation, rhythmic patterns, and
dynamics all are realized as their counterparts in attractive
movement are created. Every phrase and all larger segments
of the musical structure are "seen" as well as heard by an
observer. An advanced group of elementary children dances
out the entire third, fourth, and fifth movements of Beethoven's *Symphony No. 6,* delineating musical content in so
much detail and with such grace that the listener-onlooker
may wonder how he had theretofore missed some of what
Beethoven had to say—had missed some of the "notes." Teen-
age students listen intently to several sections of "Le Cid
Ballet Suite" by Massenet as they design attractive dances in
the Spanish style familiar to them from films and television.
Yet in these experiences nothing is "taught" in the usual
sense. Rather, children discover what is in the music in the
most natural way, and they develop finished dances just as
naturally.

The process begins with what may be for the teacher a
"loosening up" experience. She will see the children giggling
and squirming as they look at their bare feet and contemplate
the physical freedom usually not permitted in the classroom.
And the teacher should not be surprised if at first the class
does not handle this freedom well. But by continuously pointing out the desirable events, she will find that by the third
dancing time students will have an understanding of the purposes and will be aware of the joyous possibilities of ful-
filling them. Most teachers find it best to provide a large but
well-defined space for the first experience so that all members
of the class can participate at once, with no one watching.
Although on most occasions children will work best in smaller
groups, the whole-class experience is likely to be more effective in dispelling the first self-consciousness in moving freely
to music. For this occasion the teacher will select lively music
with strong rhythm and obvious contrasts. Such compositions

as "March" and "Comedian's Gallop" from *The Comedians* by Kabalevsky, the "Polka" from *Schwanda, The Bagpipe Player* by Weinberger and *Suite No. 2 for Small Orchestra* by Shostakovich are sure to catch the imagination of children. Because in this first experience many people are on the floor at once, class members will be asked to move in the same direction but urged to spread out to "cover the floor" and use the entire space. Some typical annoyances are inevitable in the beginning—children may tend to close in, using less than all of the available space; a few children may delight in bumping into others; some may be carried away with the freedom of movement and disregard the music; there may be a tendency to use only very small body movements and foot patterns. But these weaknesses disappear almost at once as children understand the genuine purposes of the activity and the pleasures of it. In a gymnasium or cleared-out classroom, chairs should be used to define the dancing space so that children cannot become "lost" and so that each person has an assigned place to sit for discussion of the event or for re-listening and thinking through sections of the music.

In a few such introductory experiences children will become comfortable with the physical freedom and will be able to experiment with large and small movements. They will experience the pleasure of relating their movements to the content of the music as they hear it. The teacher will have opportunities to comment on many aspects of the work and through comments to clarify purposes, encourage concentration on the music, and assist children in achieving varied and expressive movement. Comments such as these will occur to a teacher during the first days of the listening-dance activity.

Class, your movement followed the rhythm of the music wonderfully. The strong accents and the excitement of the rhythm were in your movements. As I watched some of you I could see the on-going pulse of the rhythm. John and Jim made something special of the accents in their leaps and twirls. Several of you danced out complete rhythm patterns in your foot patterns.

I noticed today that few of you were dancing with the same movements. Almost everyone had an original idea or developed an original variation.

Mike, I noticed that you had much more control of your movements today. That inner radar that helps you move without touching another person was working well.

Jane, I liked your big turns and swirls. Today you were able to dance with large movements as well as small.

Anne, I was proud of the way you concentrated on the music. The music seemed to flow through your mind and body as you danced.

Today, boys and girls, I feel that you really understand this way of listening to music. Not a single person was goofing. Everyone was concentrating on the music and designing his dance with it. I'm sure you are ready to divide into groups tomorrow and go on to more advanced work.

Some general plans will be helpful in preparing for further work. It is important that children dance in groups smaller than the class group most of the time. In a class of twenty-five or thirty children, three groups, and sometimes four, will function best. The teacher will wish to change group assignments often—perhaps at the end of each month, or after studying two or three compositions. At first, grouping by chance may be best, with children counting off "one," "two," "three," the "ones" becoming Group One, and so on. At other times, when the teacher is familiar with characteristic movements of individuals, she may group together the children who seem to enjoy small, intricate foot patterns, or a few who need large space for their runs and leaps, or those who are about the same physical size and who seem to enjoy working together, and so on. He will select a composition with strong appeal for each group or a composition with contrasting sections that provide expressive possibilities for the different groups. Often, as a composition is studied, the musical content will determine the grouping for movement with various sections of the composition. Another helpful technique, especially in early stages of developing the activity, is that of assigning a starting place on the floor to each child. Children usually refer to this as the "dancing place," although it really is a standing or beginning place. Confusion and many problems are avoided when the teacher can say "Children of Group One, please take your dancing places," with each child going at once to a predetermined place on the floor. This plan assures that children will begin their movement from well-spaced places, and if they face in different directions, first movement will be free of traffic jams. Having developed a framework or organization that sets the stage for further work, and having developed understanding of the activity and its purposes, a class and the teacher are ready to go into numerous experiences in listening and moving to music.

The teacher will find that in this activity a child listens much more intently and comprehends with more depth than when he sits quietly to listen. His immediate physical response is largely intuitive, yet based on details of musical content, many of which the child cannot identify or describe in any other way and which often he does not "know that he knows." One of the main functions of the teacher, therefore, is to help the child become intellectually aware of the musical content he dramatizes. For example, with Group One responding to *Toccata for Percussion,* Third Movement, by Carlos Chavez, and with the teacher and the rest of the class observing and commenting, many elements of the music will be noticed, identified, and understood even in the first experience with the composition. Questions and comments will be directed to the dancers and to the children who observe. *What was the most important element the dancers heard in the music?* (The rhythm.) *Why does it sound most important?* (The composition is played on percussion instruments.) *What did you see in the dances that has to do with rhythm?* (The people moved with the beat. John was following the accents mostly. Pamela danced out rhythm patterns. Dan danced with the kettle drums.) *Let's all listen to the music*

*again and try to discover which percussion instruments play
the composition. Each dancer should choose one instrument
whose music he will follow next time.* (Music is played as
class listens. Music is played third time as group dances.)
*What instruments did the dancers discover?* (Jim and Dan
danced with the timpani. Three other boys followed the snare
drums. Jane and Mary danced with the orchestra bells.) *You
have discovered the rhythm and the instruments. Is there no
melody or harmony in this composition?* (Discussion of
pitched percussion instruments, of timbre, of combinations
of sounds.) As Group Two prepares to take a turn at dancing
with this music, the members may be asked to decide who
will dance with each of the six types of percussion instruments in the composition. Following their dance, observation
and comments may center around the movements that seemed
to be especially good with specific sounds, the entrances and
how the dancers can anticipate them, and the fact that the
dance seemed to "begin again." *Why did the dancers return
to the movements we saw at the beginning?* (Because the
same music returns.) *How many sections are in the composition?* (Three.) *What letters can you use to indicate the
section?* (ABA) *Which section is longest?* (B) *Were the
opening and closing sections alike?* (No, the closing section
was much shorter than the first.) During the four playings of
the three-minute composition that are required for the movement and discussion described here, the entire class will have
studied the composition in considerable detail and with
pleasure and deep interest. Furthermore, because the learning process is that of discovery and includes physical as well
as mental participation, what is known will be remembered
accurately and clearly. In the experience described, the children did, in fact, "memorize" the composition.

In the listen-dance experience, two types of participation
are essential. The children often refer to the first as "warm-up
dancing." In this, they listen and dance with abandon and
with little or no preliminary listening or structuring. This
allows a child to concentrate fully and to develop his own
ideas of both music and movement. Especially, it allows for

experimentation with movement, so that the child can discover new ways to move or can refine some of his characteristic movements. The child develops a repertoire of movements that are his own and on which he can draw. Simple compositions that can be comprehended in a few hearings and highly rhythmic music that encourages large as well as small movements will be useful for warm-up dancing. Recordings of African drumming, American Indian drumming and chanting, and other ethnic music serve well. Orchestral music derived from dances is another useful category. The second type of participation requires careful analysis of a musical composition and cooperation in designing a dance that closely parallels it. Analysis of the composition usually will be developed as children move to it, but the analysis can be done also in the usual verbalization after which the dance drama is created. Usually, the class period reserved for the listendance activity will be most pleasurable and profitable when some of both the warm-up dancing and the group analytical work are included.

Movement should be as natural and untaught as possible. Natural movements of children are exceedingly beautiful and expressive. It almost never is necessary to demonstrate movements or to have them demonstrated by someone from outside the class. Instead, movement will be improved by pointing out the work of children who achieve freedom and originality. If a boy wishes to perfect his leaps, there usually will be someone in the class who leaps well and can help him. As the teacher observes the class, she often will give a signal to dancers indicating that most members of the group are invited to stop and look at the movements of some children. A good technique is to develop the understanding that when the teacher speaks a name or several names, those whose names are called will continue their dance while the others stop where they are and watch. In this way, children can see some of the most appropriate, most original, or best executed movements. Following this plan time after time, a great variety of movement will be noticed. Such a plan will encourage originality and will help children to be aware of fine execution as well as choice of appropriate movement. If a dance is to be patterned or if some part of the composition can best be interpreted through group movement, the teacher may point out movements of several children and class members may choose the movement they find most attractive as the one they all will imitate. Thus they may decide to dance a segment of the music with "Jane's step" or "Bill's pattern."

Movement can be useful in other ways than those requiring large groups and large space. With some compositions, listening and verbal analysis in usual class places will be enhanced by inviting individuals or small groups to move in spaces available in the classroom. Often these first experiments can be recalled and used later when the class is in a larger place designing the full interpretation of the composition. Sometimes it will be desirable for children to "practice" their movements. The "trapeze artists" or the "jugglers" may have good ideas for their acts with "Dance of the Comedians," which need refining and coordinating. Such work might be done in the school patio at recess or at home or in another room apart from the class. A multitude of ways, times, and places can be found for developing expressive movement once the children and teacher are accustomed to "thinking in movement."

As a device for stimulating good listening and analysis, movement can be used incidentally and briefly as well as in more complete ways. A class hearing Smetana's *The Moldau* may be livened considerably by standing and stamping, clapping, and turning with the polka section of the composition. Small children hearing the second movement of Haydn's *Symphony No. 104* (The Clock) will gain insight into the elements *rhythm* and *melody* when one child walks with the "clock rhythm" while another spins and turns with the concurrent "long, flowing melody." Young children studying the design of a three-part selection from Schumann's *Scenes from Childhood* will benefit greatly by seeing a few children in movement with the "A section," a different group in different movement with the "B section," and the first group repeating the movement with the repeated "A section." If some students have difficulty in hearing the oboe part of a recorded orchestral composition, a student who does hear it may delineate it clearly for the class by moving with it as the recording is played again.

Many musical concepts may be comprehended also when movement is used as a compositional medium. Individual students or small groups may be given assignments such as these.

Develop a "dance rondo." Use the usual sectional rondo plan for your dance. Play an accompaniment for your dance on percussion instruments.

Develop dances based on other musical forms you know. Compose variations on a movement theme without music. Later compose an accompaniment for your dance. Develop a "polyphonic" dance in the same way. Try a freer form and call your dance "Fantasia."

Develop a pattern of movement that illustrates these musical symbols. ⎯⎯ ⎯⎯ Play an accompaniment for your movements on some instrument available in your classroom.

Develop a dance with a folk song you know. Sing as you perform your dance and then perform the dance without the song.

Select a few notated rhythmic patterns. Play your patterns on a percussion instrument, and with repetitions, develop a design you like. Compose a dance with your rhythmic composition. Perform the dance with and without accompaniment.

Interpretation-dramatization of the content of music as a way of listening and analyzing is of unusual value in education. It provides for discovery of musical elements by the individual child and for delineation and expression of what he hears. Intense listening is natural and pleasurable because the response in movement depends upon it. Active participation of the child is made possible through his "performance" of music. The movement may be derived from various components of rhythm, units of pitches, phrases, sections or other units of organization, dynamics, sound sources such as instrumentation, or program notes of the composer, and these elements may be expressed singly or in combination.

In addition to the values in learning music, the activity has very rewarding human values. Remarkable personality development and behavioral changes sometimes are noted as a result of it. It allows every child to succeed. It provides an outlet for true expression and originality. It provides physical freedom that is genuine, yet acceptable in the classroom. The limits of the activity are determined by the music itself so that the finest kind of self-discipline can develop. Cooperation and ensemble feeling are natural and inevitable in the interest of creating the dance that expresses the music. I have seen a shy little girl whose self-image was that of an "ugly duckling" become very beautiful as she danced "the leading part" in a dance drama that she and her classmates composed. New dimensions in music were revealed to her, but even more important was the change in the way she felt about herself. A boy who was considered to be a behavior problem had successful experiences in "being a clown" with one piece of music and in dancing with bounding, bouncing movement in a "solo part" of another, and was reported by his teachers to be a happier child whose behavior was changed, apparently by the freedom he enjoyed and by the class recognition of the unique contribution derived from his special personality and physical characteristics. A class of children known to "hate music" and to be "uncooperative in music class" was reported to change attitude markedly after a series of successful experiences in learning musical compositions through movement.

Having said all this, I feel as Dalcroze must have felt when he said that his methods of teaching could not be conveyed through writing about them and that his writing was for those who already had participated in his classes. This article no doubt will be most helpful to those who have seen one of the demonstrations in which I have presented children at work in the listen-dance activity. Others will gain some insight from reading about it, and, I hope, will be brave enough just to begin. A few experimental lessons are sure to convince a teacher of the time-saving possibilities and of the joyous and deep musical experiences available. A summary of hints follows.

The tempo of recordings selected is exceedingly important. The natural tempo of children in movement must be recognized. A tempo that is too slow will result in heavy, lumbering movement that cannot have resilience or be satisfying. One conductor may record the minuet section of a symphony in the tempo of a lively country dance, another in the tempo of a formal ballroom dance. It is necessary in selecting a recording for analysis in movement to give special attention to tempo.

You may take different approaches to the study of music through movement. The class often will hear a composition once before dancing with it. Sometimes, however, moving with first hearing is an interesting way of discovering what is in the music. Or the children may listen more than once, discuss what they hear, and make general plans for the design of the dance before beginning the movement.

Divide the class into groups to avoid tiring and crowding of space. Involve the seated groups in observation as they (1) watch for movements that "look like the music," (2) identify elements that are realized in the movement, (3) select movements to use in the patterning of a complete dance composition, and (4) comment on what they hear in the music that is not seen in the movement. Simplify class procedures by assigning a starting place on the floor to each member of a group.

Remind children: *You will enjoy dancing more if you think of the music and not of yourselves. Try to concentrate on the music all the way through.* Use descriptive phrases to point out and encourage desirable work and a pattern for comments of children who are observing. *I can see the rhythm patterns in John's foot patterns. The legato melody of the*

*cello is in Diane's dancing. As Jim and Bob and John do their
dances again, notice the polyrhythms they hear in the music.*

Let the movement be natural. Improve movement by pointing
out freedom and originality, well executed movements, or
movements especially expressive of the music. Provide opportunities for children to refine their movements by oc-
casional practice of an idea, individually or in small groups.

Provide periods of time for warm-up dancing in which children listen and dance freely with a great variety of music,
without preliminary study and structuring, and with a mini-
mum of comment. In this time the child will concentrate deeply on the music and his own interpretation, will experiment
with original movements, and develop his own style of
movement.

Encourage individual children and groups to have favorite
"dancing music" they claim as their own. Select compositions "especially for Randy and Robert." In this way, musical
preferences as well as personality and movement characteristics can be accommodated and developed.

Provide adequate space for the type of movement you expect
to encourage. Some movement can be performed effectively
and some purposes fulfilled by children in a normal classroom environment. Group movement and most experimental
movement require a classroom with furniture pushed to the
walls or a larger room. Hampered movement is neither expressive of the music nor satisfying to the child.

There is little music that does not lend itself to choreography in the classroom, but compositions with more obvious
rhythmic and formal content will be best for early experiences at any age level. The following compositions have been
taught successfully through movement and have been the basis
for attractive finished dance performances.

Stravinsky—Suite No. 2 for Small Orchestra (March, Waltz, Polka,
    Galop)
Schumann—Scenes of Childhood
Saint-Saens—Carnival of the Animals

Cage—Dance
Mozart—German Dances
Coates—Cinderella Fantasy
Weber—Rondo for Bassoon and Orchestra
Telemann—Heroic Music
Stravinsky—Petrouchka Ballet Suite (Shrovetide Fair)
Handel—Concerto No. 25 "Water Music"
Kodaly—Hary Janos Suite (Viennese Musical Clock)
Kodaly—Hary Janos Suite (Battle and Defeat of Napoleon)
Brubeck—Unsquare Dance
Brubeck—The Riddle (Swingin' Round)
Cowell—Symphony No. 11 (Second and Fourth Movements)
Fernandez—Batuque
Bach—Suite No. 3 in D Major (Gavotte)
Vivaldi—The Seasons
Chavez—Toccata for Percussion (Third Movement)
Bizet—L'Arlesienne Suite No. 2 (Farandole)
Massenet—Le Cid Ballet Suite
Haydn—Symphony No. 94 (Third Movement)
Mussorgsky—Pictures at an Exhibition
Copland—Rodeo (Hoe-Down)
Beethoven—Symphony No. 6 (Third, Fourth, Fifth Movements)

The author of this article first introduced the school music method devised by Anna Lechner to American music educators in an article in the February 1967 issue of *Music Educators Journal*. Since the method comes from the part of the world that produced the work of Kodaly and Orff, some similarities might be expected, and they do exist. Nevertheless, it is a separate plan for early childhood that teachers studying European methods might like to know. The author recently completed an English translation of Frau Lechner's book *School Music that Lives*. He was asked to prepare this article especially for this book. It is an overview of the Lechner method with examples of materials in which German texts have been replaced with English texts.

# THE WORK OF ANNA LECHNER, VIENNESE MUSIC EDUCATOR

Stuart J. Ling

The first edition of Anna Lechner's book *Ein froher Weg ins Reich der Tone* Volume I (A Happier Road to the Realm of Tonality), was written in 1926. It took a middle ground between the old traditional methods and the extremely progressive approaches in vogue at that time. It stood on the premise that the only art that expresses the spirit and forms the character of children is that which they create from their own feelings and experience. Furthermore, it held that they must learn to use the available vocabulary of music in order to create effectively. Frau Lechner, who was a Viennese school music teacher, was thereafter engaged as a lecturer at the Pedagogical Institute of Vienna where she trained prospective music teachers. Volume 2 of her book appeared in 1931.

During World War II, the Nazis returned to more authoritarian educational procedures and the Lechner approach was temporarily abandoned. Following the war, she was once again active in teaching at the Pedagogical Institute and in demonstrating her method with children at the campus school. Both volumes of *Ein froher Weg* were revised in 1949. In 1954, after many requests from school music teachers, she published *Erlebte Schulmusik* (School Music that Lives), which presents less theory but includes a wealth of practical examples of procedure. The method was so successful, and attracted so much attention, that in 1962 (shortly after Frau Lechner's death) the city of Vienna turned an entire *Volkschule* over to a research project with the Lechner method. Elfriede Caffou, one of Frau Lechner's pupils and colleagues, was named principal and was put in charge of the instruction. In this school, work in languages, visual arts, and music were coordinated. The students were not selected on the basis of talent, but comprised the normal population of a downtown Vienna public school.

In addition to running this school and program, Frau Caffou was engaged by the Pedagogical Institute to teach the Lechner course in the evenings and in the summer. She also set up in-service training through clinic sessions held on alternate Wednesday afternoons during the school year. These were attended by public and parochial music and classroom teachers, and by visitors from all over the world. At these sessions one of her classes was used to illustrate procedures. In 1967 a second school was included in the ongoing study. Many schools, although not part of the research program, use the Lechner method either *in toto* or in combination with other approaches. The Lechner method, known also as the Viennese method, is compulsory in German Switzerland, and also is used widely in Germany. The materials have been translated into Spanish, and the method has won acceptance in Spain and in some South American countries.

The Lechner method is intended for use with children in the *Volkschule*. In the United States it would be most appropriate for children between the ages of four and nine. In Austria the best results come with long (50-minute) classes every day. In America a more realistic goal might be a 30-minute daily lesson. In Austria the method is most successful in schools where one classroom teacher with a musical background does all of the music teaching. Such teachers have been trained at Frau Caffou's Institute, attending the biweekly clinic sessions after school. For these sessions Frau

Caffou uses a class of school children to illustrate procedures. Dissemination of the method has been due, in large part, to visitations of foreigners who observe Frau Caffou in action, both in the classroom and at the Institute.

The general approach of Anna Lechner is to treat music as a language. As a language, music must be expressive and communicative. It has a vocabulary, not of words so much as of ideas that are to be experienced and used. It has inflections in the physical sensation of pitch. It is organized in certain traditional ways that form the basis of expression and make communication easier. It has a written symbolization that facilitates repetition and communication. There are stresses and accents, gestures, and other body movements. There are moods affected by tempo, rhythm, intensity, timbre, and contrast. As with spoken language, music is enhanced by pictures, dramatization, and accompaniment.

The Lechner method places great emphasis on the creation of songs by the children. Frau Lechner felt that the song is the most personal musical expression for a child, since every aspect in its performance is tied to the child's body. All musical activity in the early stages grows out of this endeavor. Frau Lechner believed the singing of spontaneous melodies to be a universal and natural means of expression for young children. With this in mind she listed the six principles of her method: (1) the child moves from musical experience to musical understanding; (2) growth in musical understanding parallels the child's intellectual-emotional development; (3) the school is obligated to develop all of the child's musical talents; (4) the child's musical training should be centered on the impact of his musical experience rather than on theoretical knowledge; (5) musical appreciation of music rather than finished musicianship, should be the ultimate goal of the school music experience; and (6) the ear and the voice should be jointly and systematically developed.

*Level One*

With the youngest children there is much concentration on fantasy and movement, utilizing the appeal of rhythm and rhyme. Verses are chanted rhythmically, emphasizing expression and using the descending minor third initially, along with other notes of the pentatonic scale. The Lechner system begins in the key of D, with all starting pitches derived from a $^1$ in order to establish a muscular feeling for pitch. The work has objectives in five basic areas:

1. Rhythm. This includes rhythmic motions, rhythmic speech, and development of a feeling for measure, notes, and rests. Rhythmic motion (the up-and-down movement of a hammer, for instance) illustrates the down-up (1-2) of duple meter. Rhythmic speech includes the recitation of verses that contain particular rhythmic motifs. Over a period of time, all basic patterns of quarter notes, half notes, and rests are introduced (in 2/4, 3/4, and 4/4 meters), utilizing seasonal verses of interest to small children. Rhythm instruments are use to supplement the work, and children are encouraged to recite expressively. This helps to accentuate the rhythm and highlights communication.

2. Pitch. The children are led to think in terms of motifs rather than notes. Early songs concentrate on the descending minor third. The range is limited to $d^1$-$b^1$. The children move immediately to the improvisation of melodies once a new verse is recited. Frau Lechner's rationale was that much as we learn to put words together in the spoken language, we must learn how notes are fashioned into musical motifs or thoughts, which communicate feelings and express ideas and moods. One need not be concerned about stifling creativity. Even the most avant-garde authors and poets first learn to use the traditional mother-tongue in a common everyday manner.

3. Pitch Symbolization. Sounds come before symbols, and may be represented in many ways. Familiar items are used to demonstrate pitch variation:
Church bells:

bim  — $a^1$
bahm — $f\#^1$
boom — $d^1$

Christmas tree ornaments:

To reinforce the pitch relationships, a system of hand signals or air-writing is recommended. These differ from the Kodaly signals in that they are related to the head, the area where sound resonates and is focused. The basic signals involve the placement of the outstretched hand (palm down) as follows:

$b^1$ — at the hairline
$a^1$ — at the forehead
$g^1$ — at the eyes
$f\#^1$ — at the tip of the nose
$e^1$ — at the mouth
$d^1$ — at the chin

4. Pitch Recognition and Reading. The first objective is grasp of the melodic shape of a motif. Listening games are used in order to help build a vocabulary of musical motifs and to test motif recognition. The "Mouse Dance" is an example of this:

The class is divided into four groups. Each group is assigned a particular dance picture (each in a different color). When the teacher sings one of the motifs on a neutral syllable, the appropriate group of mice begins to dance. There are numerous versions of this basic game using flowers, balls, leaves, and so on. The children are encouraged to invent subjects for this kind of play, which helps to build associations between sound and symbol.

5. Form. The earliest emphasis is on simple imitation using questions and answers. For example, the teacher sings "What does mother do?" and the children are encouraged to

improvise answers such as "Cleans around the house," "Cooks a dinner too," "Mends your socks for you."

*Level Two*

At this level children are still creatures of fantasy and function, interested in things and feelings. The texts of children's folk music constitute the most suitable material. The upward range is extended to $d^2$ (hand signal just above the head), with the leading tone bypassed for the present. All previous activities continue and are strengthened. The process of turning sound-pictures into note-pictures begins to reverse. The specific objectives are as follows:

1. Rhythm. More complicated patterns are introduced, featuring mixtures of motifs both with and without pickup beats. Texts suggesting large body motions should be selected. A typical rhythmic verse might be "The lion walks on padded paws / The squirrel leaps from limb to limb / While flies can crawl straight on the wall / And seals can dive and swim."

2. Pitch. The complete scale is used, and the variations in patterns include both ascending and descending skips of the third, fourth, fifth, octave, and triad motifs. The children move into the key of G using common harmonies.

3. Note Writing and Reading. Sound-pictures are changed into note-pictures with the help of hand signals, and vice versa. Some attempts are made to read directly from notation.

4. Strengthening Pitch Relationships. This is accomplished by means of the following steps:

(a) Continuation of optical-acoustical play.

(b) Identification of changes in sound pictures. By way of illustration, the following game may be played. The teacher places on the board:

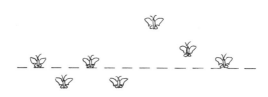

Of course this is:

However, the teacher sings:

Pret - ty    lit - tle    but - ter - fly.

and asks the children which butterfly has gotten lost. There are many possible variations. This kind of activity places demands on both aural and musical judgment, and is really the beginning of interval recognition.

(c) Recognition of familiar songs from sound pictures (song puzzles). The following illustrates the manner in which children at this level participate in solving a song puzzle:

The teacher draws attention to the above, which appears on the chalkboard, and asks the students to identify it. "A song." "A strange song." "One section of 3-beat in the middle of

4-beat music." "Two double bars in the middle." "Part of several songs." Teacher: "Bravo! You are good at solving puzzles. This is a song puzzle. In fact there are four of them, each a part of a song we know." The teacher sings the third on la and asks, "Which one did I sing and what was its name?" One child will suggest perhaps the second. "Why can that not be?" "Because you have not sung any half notes . . . because you have not sung any leaps . . . because you haven't sung any high notes . . ." and so on. Eventually they will choose the proper song.

(d) Recognition and singing of unfamiliar motifs.

(e) Sight-reading of easy songs.

5. Form. Concentration is placed upon the following elements:

(a) Two- and three-part song form.

(b) Form extension and consequent phrases.

(c) Simple imitation.

The children deal with these in both the songs that they compose and those they learn by rote or attempt to sight-read. They should feel and identify four-, eight-, twelve-, and sixteen-measure groupings, and be able to differentiate between full measure phrases and those that include pickup notes.

*Level Three*

Children at this level generally look at things more realistically. Intellectual activities become more important. There is some concentration on the more formal and technical aspects of music as found in the folksong. Every song is made of phrases and not just notes written on the paper. When the phrase is recognized, it can be read from the page. The children should begin to analyze the rhythmic patterns, motifs, and forms that make up a folksong. This child's music, like his language, will be appropriate for his age level. The work includes:

1. Rhythm. Review of known values. Concentration on patterns including eighth notes, rests, dotted rhythms, and combined patterns.

2. Pitch. There should be security in D and G Major, and some work in C Major. The vocal range is widened to $c^1$-$e^2$. There is more awareness of motifs. The children should begin to sing what the teacher indicates with hand signals. Melodies should express words, with important syllables accented by skips, for instance.

3. Singing from Notation. Frau Lechner suggests a game where the hunting dogs (students) chase the rabbit (teacher) up and down the hills:

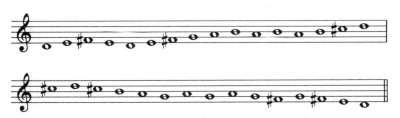

The teacher uses a pointer, and may go forward, backward, or skip around. Certain key pitches are given additional symboys. The pitch $a^1$ is a tree, where the tired dogs may rest. Low $d^1$ is a brook in a valley, where they may pause for refreshment. The $f\#^1$ is a hunting lodge, another resting place. High $d^2$ is a hilltop. These symbols emphasize the tonic triad.

4. Form. In dealing with form, both rhythmic and melodic motifs are considered. An example of this follows:

This is a graphic representation of:

The  au-tumn  leaves are  fall - ing, the  sum-mer's gone  a - way,

The birds are  fly - ing   to  the south, they'll  all  be  back next May.

From this the children may note that (a) each motif has a different set of leaves, (b) there are four motifs, (c) the first and third motifs are almost alike, (d) their leaves are the same color, (e) the second and fourth are different but similar, (f) the first and third are like arches, (g) the second is like stairsteps, (h) the fourth is similar to the second but has skips at the end, (i) all motifs start with the same pitch, (j) the second and fourth have the same number of leaves, (k) the first, second, and fourth each have a big leaf, and (l) the high point, or climax, is in the third motif.

The children learn how a melody is made using repetition, transposition (sequence), reversal, expansion, and diminution. The teacher sings musical motifs to which the children supply repeated, transposed, reversed, expanded and diminished motifs. The harmonic aspects of form are confronted in the creation of canons and rounds. An example:

Another technique for creating a melody is the use of melisma. This is an exciting way to change a tune so that the music better fits the words.

Before: Out on the wat - er the la - zy ship floats.

After:

Melodic analysis is done in the following fashion:

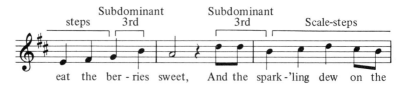

eat the ber-ries sweet, And the spark-'ling dew on the

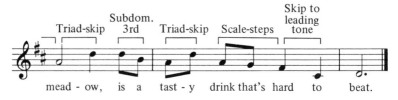

mead-ow, is a tast-y drink that's hard to beat.

The rhythmic aspects of form are explored through "puzzles" such as the following:

"Complete these rhythmic patterns:"

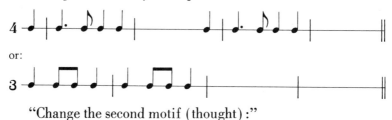

or:

"Change the second motif (thought):"

"Answer with a second line that fits the following line:"

The preceding may be done with clapping, tapping, or with percussion instruments.

*Level Four*

Children at this level are much more observant and independent. Emphasis is placed on musical-artistic development, establishment of the feeling for tonality, and two-part singing of folksongs. The work is as follows:

1. Rhythm. The eighth note is used as a counting note, as in 3/8, 4/8, and 6/8 meters. Rhythmic canons are clapped.

2. Pitch. The key of F Major is introduced. Work with basic I-IV-V-I sequences involves the singing of cadence melodies:

The dominant-seventh harmony is introduced, and the tendencies of certain pitches are illustrated in the resolution to tonic harmony:

Melodies are analyzed in the following manner: T=tonic, D=dominant, S=subdominant.

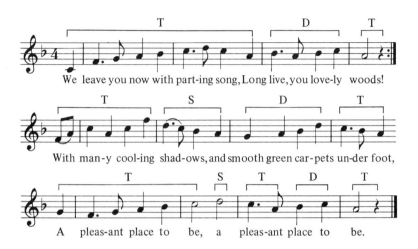

Two-part singing includes (a) singing in thirds, (b) singing typical cadential endings, (c) using the horn "quint," (d) singing in sixths, and (e) using combinations of the above. The harmony is analyzed and compared to a pendulum, moving from tonic to subdominant, back through tonic to dominant, and resting in the tonic.

3. Voice Building. A few important guidelines should be considered: (a) Voice Placement. Beware of a lazy mouth. Distinguish between open and closed vowels. Sing vowels long and consonants short. Do not overlook consonants. (b) Breath Control. Utilize a stream of air. Use all of the lungs. Conserve air. Breathe in the proper places. Avoid too much air pressure. (c) Tone Building. Sing without exertion. Keep the throat open and relaxed. Make the vowel sound resonant. Feel the tone forward. Try for a uniform sound.

In a recent article appearing in the Austrian journal *Musik Erziehung*, Frau Caffou defends a strong emphasis on teaching of integrated arts, which is at the heart of the Lechner method. These arts include, in Frau Caffou's opinion, music, graphic arts, language, and certain aspects of physical education. She claims that the deemphasis of these in modern schools will result in a stultification of the child's emotional development, a decrease in imagination (so necessary for scientific discovery), a reduction in healthy social interplay, and a lessening of the societal aspects of civilization. Frau Caffou claims that we need freedom from tensions and that this comes about when children know how to express themselves creatively through the arts. She feels that young people sense this, and react against being turned into robots, sometimes in a destructive way. Frau Caffou agrees with those who see a misplacement of values in society as contributing to juvenile crime, and urges the schools to include opportunities to learn correct values, which are integral to the arts.

Furthermore, she urges that the schools provide an artistic environment. The kind of beauty she talks about is more than new buildings. It should involve an awareness and responsibility on the part of the children. The atmosphere of the school should be one of unforced serenity, which affects both the work done and the social interaction.

Among the things the students can do is to create the works of art that decorate their rooms and building, concentrating on the use of colors and shapes to express moods and attitudes about what is current and important to them. They should be encouraged to improve their language usage by conscious effort to choose words and phrases that are more expressive. They should be given opportunity to improvise scenes that involve everyday events in order to focus on their feelings and the expression of these feelings. Lastly, they should be constantly involved in composing songs about any number of things including seasons, special occasions, people, pets, and commonplace events. In other words, the arts need to become something that people use in a very practical way for the purpose of making them more human.

It is extremely important that everyone be given an opportunity to participate. Frau Caffou states that any activity is only as valuable to an individual as that person's involvement in it. We can help to develop a sense of self-worth in children by affording opportunities for them to be creative, and by helping each child to develop the necessary creative skills.

# ADDITIONAL READING

# DALCROZE

## Books

Aronoff, Frances Webber. *Music and Young Children.* New York: Holt, Rinehart & Winston, Inc., 1969.

Brown, Margaret, and Betty K. Sommer. *Movement Education: Its Evolution and a Modern Approach.* Reading, Massachusetts: Addison-Wesley Publishing Co., 1969.

Driver, Ann. *Music and Movement.* London: Oxford University Press, 1936. Available from Oxford University Press, 1600 Pollitt Drive, Fair Lawn, New Jersey 07010.

Driver, Ethel. *A Pathway to Dalcroze Eurhythmics.* 1951. Reprinted edition, London: Thomas Nelson and Sons, 1963.

Findlay, Elsa. *Rhythm and Movement: Applications of Dalcroze Eurhythmics.* Evanston, Illinois: Summy-Birchard, 1971.

Freeman, Roslyn W. *Motion and Music for the Maladjusted.* Brooklyn: Freeman Publishing Co., 1949.

Gell, Heather. *Music, Movement and the Young Child.* Sydney: Australasian Publishing Company, 1949. Available from Lawrence Verry, Inc., 16 Holmes Street, Mystic, Connecticut 06355.

Jaques-Dalcroze, Emile. *Rhythmic Movement.* London: Novello and Co., Ltd., 1920-1921, 2 vols.

———. *Rhythm, Music and Education.* Translated from the French by Harold F. Rubinstein. Abridged Reprint Edition. London & Whitstable: The Riverside Press, Ltd., 1967.

## Articles and Studies

Aronoff, Frances W. "Games Teachers Play: Dalcroze Eurythmics," *Music Educators Journal,* Vol. 57 (February 1971), pp. 28-32.

Baker, M. "Bibliography: Books on Eurhythmics and Some Music," *Etude,* Vol. 65 (October 1947), p. 544.

Barr, G. "Rhythm and the child," *School Arts,* Vol. 44 (February 1945), pp. 192-195.

Berlin-Papish, T. "Some Uses of the Dalcroze Method in Piano Teaching," *Piano Teacher,* Vol. 7 (May 1965), pp. 8-11.

Boepple, Paul. "The Study of Rhythm," *Yearbook of the Music Supervisors National Conference,* 1931, pp. 192-194.

Brody, Viola A. "The Role of Body-Awareness in the Emergence of Musical Ability," *Journal of Research in Music Education,* Vol. 1 (Spring 1953), p. 17.

Clarke, U. "Dalcroze: Rhythm in a Chain Reaction," *Musical America,* Vol. 70 (November 15, 1950), p. 25.

Gehrkens, Karl W. "A Page or Two of Opinion," *Educational Music Magazine,* Vol. 29 (September-October 1949), pp. 11-13.

————. "Why Not Eurhythmics?" *Etude*, Vol. 72 (May 1954), p. 22.

Glenn, Mabelle. "Demonstration of Creative Rhythm," *Yearbook of the Music Supervisors National Conference*, 1932, pp. 311-314.

————. "Trends in Music Education," *Yearbook of the Music Supervisors National Conference*, 1933, pp. 258-262.

Grentzer, Rose Marie. "Eurhythmics in the Elementary School Program," *Etude*, Vol. 62 (January 1944), p. 22.

Hall, Lucy Duncan. "The Value of Eurhythmics in Education," *Yearbook of the Music Educators National Conference*, 1936, pp. 150-153.

Jagger, M. B. "Music is Everywhere," *Parents Magazine*, Vol. 22 (April 1947), p. 31.

Jaques-Dalcroze, Emile. "The Child and the Pianoforte," trans. F. Rothwell, *Musical Quarterly*, Vol. 14 (April 1928), pp. 203- 215.

————. "Dalcroze Explains his Method," *Literary Digest*, Vol. 78 (September 1923), pp. 31-32.

Kestenberg, Leo. "Music Education Goes Its Own Way," *Musical Quarterly*, Vol. 25 (October 1939), pp. 447-448.

Maier, Guy. "The Teacher's Round Table," *Etude* (May 1941), p. 310.

Martin, Frank. "Eurhythmics: The Jaques-Dalcroze Method," *Music in Education*. International Conference on the Role and Place of Music in the Education of Youth and Adults (Brussels, June 29-July 9, 1953). Soleure, Switzerland: UNESCO, 1955.

Mendel, A. "Mental and Bodily Rhythm," *Nation*, Vol. 134 (February 17, 1932), p. 210.

Naumberg, M. "The Dalcroze Idea: What Eurhythmics Is and What it Means," *Outlook*, Vol. 106 (January 17, 1914), pp. 127-131.

Rosenstrauch, Henrietta. *Percussion, Movement and the Child*. Far Rockaway, New York: Carl Van Roy Co., 1964.

————. "Rhythmic Problems in Music Teaching," *Volume of Proceedings of the Music Teachers National Association*, 1946, pp. 342-349.

Scholl, Sharon. "Music for Dancers," *Music Educators Journal*, Vol. 52 (February-March 1966), pp. 99-102.

Schuster, Hilda M. *Dalcroze Eurhythmics*. Masters thesis, Duquesne University School of Music, 1938.

————. "Dalcroze Exceptions: Reply to U. Clarke," *Musical America*, Vol. 70 (December 15, 1950), p. 12.

The Dalcroze School of Music
Hilda M. Schuster, Director
161 East 73rd Street
New York, N.Y. 10021

# KODALY

## Books

Adam, Jeno. *Growing in Music with Movable Do*. Edited by Georgiana Peterson; trans. by Louis Boros, Joseph Held, and Louis Munkachy. Copyright 1971 by Louis Boros, 359D Crowells Park, Highland Park, New Jersey 08904.

Bacon, Denise. *Let's Sing Together: Songs for 3, 4, and 5 year olds from Mother Goose and Others Set to Music According to the Kodaly Concept*. Wellesley, Massachusetts: Kodaly Musical Training Institute, Inc., 1971.

Eosze, Laszlo. *Kodaly: His Life in Pictures*. Boston: Crescendo Publishing Co., 1972.

————. *Zoltan Kodaly: His Life and Work*. Boston: Crescendo Publishing Co., 1962.

Kersey, Robert. *Just Five*, a collection of pentatonic songs. Westminster, Maryland: The Westminster Press.

————. *Just Five Plus Two* (fa and ti are added). Westminster, Maryland: The Westminster Press.

Sandor, Frigyes. *Musical Education in Hungary*. Budapest: Corvina, Second revised edition, 1969.

Szabo, Helga. *The Kodaly Concept of Music Education*. English edition by Geoffry Russell-Smith. London: Boosey & Hawkes, Ltd., 1969. Textbook with 3 LP records. Available from Boosey & Hawkes, 209 Victor Street, Oceanside, New York 11572.

Young, Percy M. *Zoltan Kodaly, A Hungarian Musician*. London: Ernest Benn, 1964.

## Articles and Studies

Adam, Jeno. "The Influence of Folk Music on Public Musical Education in Hungary," *Studia Musicologica*, Vol. 7 (1965), pp. 10-18.

Bacon, Denise. "The Why of Kodaly," *Music Journal*, Vol. 29, No. 7 (September 1971), p. 26.

Borszormenyi-Nagy, Bela. "The Kodaly Legacy," *Clavier*, Vol. 7 (September 1968), pp. 16-17.

Daniel, Katinka. "The Kodaly Method," *Clavier*, Vol. 7 (September 1968), pp. 20-21.

Darazs, Arpad. "The Kodaly Method for Choral Training," *American Choral Review*, Vol. 8, No. 3 (1966), pp. 8-12.

DiBonaventura, M. "Zoltan Kodaly: Man and Mountain," *Pan Pipes*, Vol. 58, No. 3 (1966), pp. 15-16. Also in *Council for Research in Music Education Bulletin*, No. 8 (Fall 1966), p. 59.

Edwards, L. "Hungary's Musical Powerline to the Young," *Music Educators Journal*, Vol. 57 (February 1971), p. 38.

Erdely, Stephen. *Methods and Principles of Hungarian Ethnomusicology.* Bloomington, Indiana: Indiana University Publications.

Kokas, Klara. "Psychological Testing in Hungarian Music Education," *Journal of Research in Music Education,* Vol. 17 (Spring 1969), pp. 125-134.

Moll, Elizabeth M. "The Significance of the Kodaly Concept in America," *Musart,* Vol. 22 (April-May 1970).

Ringer, A. L. "Lives of Kodaly," *Saturday Review* (July 31, 1962), pp. 33-34.

Steen, Phillip L. "Zoltan Kodaly's Choral Music for Children and Youth Choirs," Doctoral Dissertation, University of Michigan, 1970.

Stone, Margaret L. "Kodaly and Orff Music Teaching Techniques: History and Present Practice," Doctoral Dissertation, Kent State University, 1971.

Szabolsci, Bence. "Kodaly and Universal Education," *Studia Musicologica,* Vol. 3 (1962), pp. 7-9.

Szonyi, Erzsebet. "Zoltan Kodaly's Pedagogic Activities," *International Music Educator* (March 1966), pp. 418-420.

Young, Percy M. "Zoltan Kodaly—Pioneer in Music Education," *Clavier,* Vol. 6, No. 4 (1967), p. 58.

Zemke, Sister Lorna. "A Comparison of the Effects of a Kodaly-Adapted Music Instruction Sequence and a More Typical Sequence on Auditory Musical Achievement in Fourth Grade Students," Doctoral Dissertation, University of Southern California, 1970.

Lectures

Forrai, Katalin. "The Practical Realization of Kodaly's Concepts of Music Education," unpublished lecture delivered at Dana School of Music Summer Course, 1969.

Nemesszeghy, Marta. "The Importance of a Daily Music Curriculum in Total Education," unpublished lecture delivered at University of Bridgeport Summer Course, 1971.

Kokas, Klara. "Psychological Tests in Connection with Music Education in Hungary," an address presented at the International Seminar on Experimental Research in Music Education, The University of Reading, England, July 9-16, 1968.

Szonyi, Erzsebet. "The International Significance of the Kodaly Method," unpublished lecture delivered at University of Bridgeport Summer Course, 1971.

Kodaly Musical Training Institute
Denise Bacon, Musical and Educational Director
525 Worcester Street
Wellesley, Massachusetts 02181

# ORFF

Books

Liess, Andreas. *Carl Orff*, trans. Adelheide and Herbert Parkin. New York: St. Martin's Press, 1966.

Thomas, Werner, et al. *Carl Orff: A Report in Words and Pictures*, Mainz, Germany: B. Schott's Sohne, 1955.

*Orff-Institute Year Books 1962, 1963, 1964-1968*, Mainz, Germany: B. Schott's Sohne.


Articles and Studies

Bacon, Denise. "On Using Orff with Kodaly," *Musart*, Vol. 21 (April-May 1969), p. 45.

Baker, K. "Orff-Schulwerk in Australia with Sub-Normal Children," *Orff-Schulwerk Society Bulletin*, No. 15 (April 1968).

Bates, K. "Creative Music with First Year Juniors," *Orff-Schulwerk Society Bulletin*, No. 4, (June 1965).

Breuer, Robert. "The Magic World of Carl Orff," *Music Journal*, Vol. 15 (March 1957), p. 56.

Burkart, Arnold. "Orff-Schulwerk in Our Schools: Toward a Pedagogical Construct," *Indiana Musicator* (January 1969).

Caddock, DeWayne G. "The Preschooler Discovers Music," *The Orff Echo*, Vol. 2 (June 1970), p. 1.

Carley, Isabel. "Music with a Difference," *The Orff Echo*, Vol. 1 (June 1969), p. 3.

Castren, David. "Orff and Junior High Percussion," *The Orff Echo*, Vol. 1 (June 1969), p. 7.

Daniel, O. "The New German Music—1959," *Saturday Review*, Vol. 42 (June 27, 1959), p. 38.

Danziger, Harris. "Orff Brings Theories to Canada," *New York Times* (August 12, 1962).

————. "Body and Song," *Opera News*, Vol. 32 (January 13, 1968), p. 8.

Ferguson, Nancy. "Orff with the Perceptually Handicapped Child," *The Orff Echo*, Vol. 2 (June 1970), p. 1.

Frank, Paul L. "Improvisation as a Teaching Device," *Triad* (January 1962).

Helm, Everett. "Carl Orff," *The Musical Quarterly*, Vol. 41 (July 1955), p. 285.

Nash, Grace C. "Kodaly and Orff," *Clavier*, Vol. 7 (September 1968), p. 18.

————. "Music in the Elementary Classroom," *Musart*, Vol. 22 (April-May 1970), p. 39.

————. "The New Music for Musicality," *Musart* (November-

December 1966).

⸺. "Orff," *The Instrumentalist,* Vol. 19 (October 1965), p. 47.

Neidig, Kenneth L. "Orff Clinic," *Bluegrass Music News,* Vol. 19 (December 1967), p. 2.

Nichols, Elizabeth. "Adapting Orff to the Music Series," *The Orff Echo,* Vol. 2 (February 1970), p. 2.

⸺. "Improvisation: Key to Orff Schulwerk," *The Orff Echo,* Vol. 2 (June 1970), p. 4.

⸺. "Instituting Movement with Children," *The Orff Echo,* (June 1970), p. 4.

⸺. "Music for the Deaf," *The Orff Echo,* Vol. 1 (June 1969), p. 4.

⸺. "Orff Can Work in Every Classroom," *Music Educators Journal,* Vol. 57 (September 1970), p. 43.

Peterson, A. Viola. "Orff and Kodaly Influences in Music Education," *The Rimer,* Vol. 1, No. 1 (October 1968), pp. 11-12.

Pleasants, Henry. "The Orff Hypothesis," *High Fidelity Magazine,* Vol. 6 (October 1956), p. 68.

⸺. "The Emergence of Orff," *Saturday Review,* Vol. 36 (September 26, 1953), p. 68.

Ponath, Louise, and Carol H. Bitcon. "A Behavioral Analysis of Orff-Schulwerk," *Journal of Music Therapy,* Vol. 9 (Summer 1972), pp. 56-63.

Schmidt, Lloyd. "Project Orff: Music for Retarded Children, Project Report 1970-1971," Hartford: Connecticut State Department of Education, 1971.

Steinberg, Carl M. "Master-Class Session for the Music Makers of Tomorrow," *High Fidelity Magazine,* Vol. 9 (June 1959).

Walter, Arnold. "Elementary Music Education: the European Approach," *Canadian Music Journal,* Vol. 2 (Spring 1958), p. 12.

⸺. "The Orff Schulwerk in American Education," *The Orff Echo,* Vol. 1, Supplement No. 3 (May 1969).

Warner, Brigitte. "Creative Play-Acting with Children," *The Orff Echo,* Vol. 1 (June 1969), p. 1.

Welsh, J. Robert. "Piano: Orff-Kodaly," *Musart,* Vol. 22 (April-May 1970), p. 40.

Wilmouth, Jean Jr. "Let Children Move," *The Orff Echo,* Vol. 2 (February 1970), p. 5.

American Orff-Schulwerk Association
Arnold E. Burkart, Executive Secretary
School of Music
Ball State University
Muncie, Indiana 47306

# SELECTED EXCERPTS FROM PUBLISHED ADAPTATIONS

### Activities: Dynamics

The children walk vigorously, beating their small drums. They lift their knees high. They walk on tiptoes and beat their drums very quietly when the music changes to pianissimo.

The children clap freely and vigorously around their bodies, assuming any position they wish. They interpret the dynamic changes expressed at the keyboard.

The children run (♫♫♫♩). On the last beat, which

is accented, they make a strong movement. They should be encouraged to invent new movements each time the pattern is repeated. As a variation, the teacher may play the six eighth notes while the children wait for the accent, at which time they make their strong movement. They hold this strong position until the accented beat is repeated in the following measure.

The children jump vigorously in all directions to the tune of "This Old Man." Words, such as "Jumping

here, jumping there, Jumping here and everywhere," may be added.

The class stands in a small circle, holding hands. The music begins quietly, the children responding with small steps. As the crescendo develops, they enlarge their steps and extend their arms. They reverse their movement for the decrescendo.

A hoop is laid on the floor. The children, sitting on their feet, grasp the hoop with both hands. As the teacher develops a crescendo in eight beats or more, the children slowly lift themselves onto their knees, raising the hoop at the same time. At the climax they

are on their knees with the hoop high above their heads. For the decrescendo, they reverse the movement until they are back at the starting position. To give variation to this experience, three hoops may be used simultaneously but in canon. For this purpose, nine beats must be used for the crescendo and nine for the decrescendo: Hoop No. 1 begins on the first count; Hoop No. 2, on the fourth count; Hoop No. 3, on the seventh count.

"Activities: Dynamics" from Elsa Findlay, *Rhythm and Movement: Applications of Dalcroze Eurhythmics* (Evanston, Illinois: Summy-Birchard Company, 1971), pp.12-15. Used by permission.

## Activities: Duration

The class walks in quarter notes, accompanied by the teacher at the keyboard, or she may use her drum. As soon as the children hear the music change to eighth notes, they stop and clap. When the rhythm changes to walking again, they immediately resume their walk. Triplets, sixteenths and skipping may also be used as the signal to stop and clap. If space is unavailable, the children may sit at their desks and clap instead of walking.

Divide the class into two groups, one representing the walking rhythm, the other, the running rhythm. Each responds to the rhythm of the music played.

The teacher stands in front of the chart, pointing to one of the rhythms displayed. The class claps the rhythm. A child stands to one side and claps the fundamental beat. A child may take the teacher role. This activity should not be given until all the rhythms on the chart have been mastered.

The children move across the room with long strides (half notes), swinging their arms in contrary motion. Emphasis should be on the stretch involved.

The children sit on their feet. If the teacher plays walking notes (quarter notes), they beat on their knees. If she plays eighth notes, they clap above their heads. When she plays half notes, they clap behind their backs. When she plays a whole note, they beat on the floor.

The children walk, run, or skip four beats, then stop and clap four beats in strict rhythm.

The class is arranged in three circles. Circle A walks, B runs, and C skips. At command, they change

# RHYTHM CHART 1

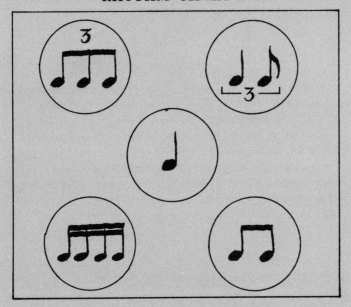

rhythms. If drums of different pitch are available, these may be used as accompaniment.

The children sit and clap quarter notes. The teacher calls 2, 3, or 4. This is a signal for them to clap either two eighths, a triplet, or four sixteenths to a beat. At command, the children resume the fundamental beat. As they master this experience, the teacher may ask them to subdivide the following beat *once* only. Since this is a very difficult exercise, only older children should be asked to attempt it, and then only after they have mastered the rhythms on Rhythm Chart 1.

"Activities: Duration" from Elsa Findlay, *Rhythm and Movement: Applications of Dalcroze Eurhythmics* (Evanston, Illinois: Summy-Birchard Company, 1971), pp.19,21-22. Used by permission.

## Activities: Meter

The class interprets a pattern of twos (2/4) by step, hop; a pattern in threes (3/4) by step, hop, hop; a pattern in fours (4/4) by step, hop, hop, hop; a pattern in fives (5/4) by step, hop, hop, hop, hop. They clap on the first beat of each pattern. When coordination has been established, two patterns may be combined: step, hop, followed by step, hop, hop (2/4 and 3/4). As a variation, the children may move forward for step, hop, and turn for step, hop, hop. The children may suggest other variations.

This exercise is called "Drum Swing," and small hand drums are used for its interpretation. The children bend forward, holding their drums in their left hands, arms at their sides. On the count of one, they swing their arms upward; on the count of two, they beat their drums with their right hands; on

1          2          3

three, arms and torso drop down easily into the starting position. As soon as the three swing has been mastered, another beat on the drum may be added, making this a four swing. Again a third beat may be added on the drum, making this a five swing. A percussion accompaniment is appropriate.

"Activities: Meter" from Elsa Findlay, *Rhythm and Movement: Applications of Dalcroze Eurhythmics* Evanston, Illinois: Summy-Birchard Company, 1971), pp.31-32. Used by permission.

## Activities: Speech and Rhythm Patterns

The children sit in a large circle, beating their drums and saying the words "Beat my drum" ( ♩♪♪ ). The teacher, beating her drum and speaking along with the class, dramatizes the words by speaking slowly, quickly, softly, or loudly. The teacher must be sure that the children imitate her changes of dynamics and tempo in strict rhythm.

Using the same words, the teacher beats her drum first, followed immediately by the class, who imitate her changing speed and dynamics.

After "Beat my drum" has been mastered, a second speech pattern using triplets may be used. "What a big room" ( ♪♪♪♩ ) lends itself well. The teacher or the children may want to use other patterns. They should always be encouraged to do so if this furthers rhythmic expression.

After much experience with the six speech patterns, the teacher "plays" one of the patterns for the children to recognize. She will note that only a few children will recognize which of the speech patterns she plays. The transfer from the drum to the keyboard is difficult for little children. From now on the speech patterns give way to melodic patterns, and the children are asked to sing along as the teacher plays the rhythms of the speech patterns.

Finally, the symbols for the six patterns are presented to the class. For this the teacher should prepare six pieces of cardboard on which the rhythms are noted. The process of learning and identifying the symbols is now underway. As the teacher presents each one, the children are asked to "spell out" the rhythms, saying the words of the speech pattern while pointing to the symbols which match them. Pointing must be from left to right.

*Concurrently with the above experiences, the following activities may be introduced:*

"One, two, buckle my shoe" may be used to good effect in the following manner. Have the children chant the rhyme and clap while noting the rhythm:

One, two, buckle my shoe; ( ♩ ♩ ♫♫ )

Three, four, close the door; ( ♩ ♩ ♫♩ )

Five, six, pick up sticks; ( ♩ ♩ ♫♩ )

Seven, eight, close the gate; ( ♩ ♩ ♫♩ )

Nine, ten, big fat hen. ( ♩ ♩ ♫♩ )

The children will discover that only the first line differs in rhythm from the others. They step the rhythm, then write it on the chalkboard.

"Activities: Speech and Rhythm Patterns" from Elsa Findlay, *Rhythm and Movement: Applications of Dalcroze Eurhythmics* (Evanston, Illinois: Summy-Birchard Company, 1971), pp.37-38.

## Activities: Rhythm and Melody

The children, sitting close to the piano, move their arms upward when the melody ascends and downward when the melody descends.

The children are arranged in a circle or a line. They follow the teacher's ascending or descending melody by kneeling or standing. The movement should be slow.

Eight children stand side by side. They pretend to be ringing church bells by pulling on ropes. Each child represents and sings a note of the scale. This sequence is appropriate: 8642-7531-87654321.

Two children stand at opposite corners of the room. The first child sings a message to the second, making up his own tune. The second must improvise an answer. For instance, one may sing, "Can you come over and play?" The second may answer, "I've got to go shopping with mother." Later, the words may be omitted as the children improvise "question and answer" melodies.

Each note of the scale is indicated by an appropriate arm position in space. The arm, held close to the body at the beginning, moves scalewise, up or down, from the first to the eighth note of the scale and the eighth to the first. The space must be accurately divided, with the fifth degree of the scale exactly at shoulder level. As the children master this melodic interpretation, they are asked to place their arms in any position which the teacher suggests, such as 1 2 3 2 1 or 1 2 3 4 5 8. This can become more complicated with the interpretation of a simple song like "Twinkle, Twinkle, Little Star." The children should always sing as they move their arms up and down. The first, third, fifth, and eighth notes of the scale should receive particular emphasis.

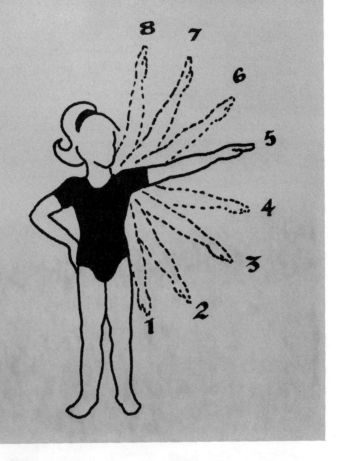

"Activities: Pitch and Melody" from Elsa Findlay, *Rhythm and Movement: Applications of Dalcroze Eurhythmics* (Evanston, Illinois: Summy-Birchard Company, 1971), pp.51-52. Used by permission.

## Activities: Movement and Space Patterns

The children design a circle, a square, a triangle, a star, the face of a clock, etc. They may do this in groups, and any number may participate. They may stand, kneel, or lie on the ground. They should touch hands or feet at some point.

Three children stand side by side, holding hands. One assumes a position on the first of four beats, the second improvises a complementary movement on the

second beat, followed by the third child's movement on the third beat. They hold their "picture" for the fourth beat. The children must be aware of how the designs are developing and changing.

The children run, then freeze when the music stops. They must find new positions each time they freeze.

The group designs a picture. The children number off. No. 1 takes the central part of the picture and assumes a position. Then each child in turn improvises a movement which will contribute to the total picture. When everyone has added his movement, the children must evaluate the design they have created.

"Activities: Movement and Space Patterns" from Elsa Findlay, *Rhythm and Movement: Applications of Dalcroze Eurhythmics* (Evanston, Illinois: Summy-Birchard Company, 1971), pp.65-66. Used by permission.

## GOOD MORNING

S - L - S, M - R - M

C pentatonic

Grace C. Nash

Good morn-ing, Good morn-ing, How are you? I'm
(Good- bye now, Good- bye now, Keep well now, Keep

fine - It's good to sing to - geth-er, In an - y kind of weath-er, To
well now, I'm glad we've been to - geth-er, Re-gard-less of the weath-er, But

start the day a - long, a - long, In song, In song, to - geth-er.
now we'll say,"so long, so long", In song, In song, to - geth-er. )

*Suggestions:* The song can be introduced as an echo-answer song with teacher singing the first phrase, the class answering with the second phrase. Later divide the class, and one group can sing the teacher's part. Before the instruments are used, try only Guitar accompaniment, tapping across the strings, on the beat, with a dowel (claves) stick or pencil.

*Introduction:* The instruments are numbered according to their entrance (2 bars apart). Clapping, (alternate hand-on-top, right, left, right, etc.) will begin with the entrance of Soprano Bells and continue to the end of song.

After the song is finished, the instruments may continue playing 4 or more bars. Explore other tone patterns on the instruments to accompany the song.

230

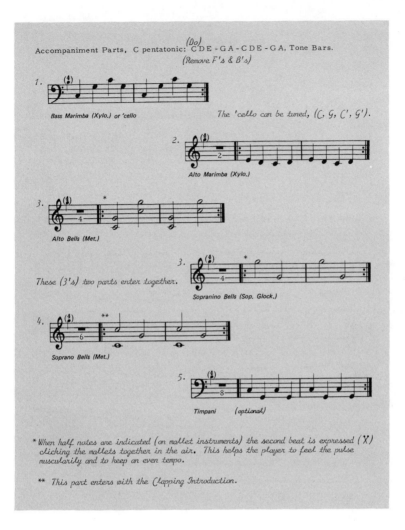

"Good Morning" from Grace Nash, *Music with Children, Series I* (LaGrange, Illinois: Kitching Educational, 1965), pp.12-13. Used by permission of Grace Nash.

231

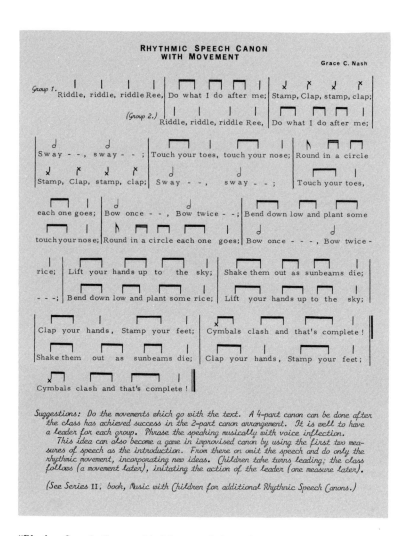

# RHYTHMIC SPEECH CANON
## WITH MOVEMENT

Grace C. Nash

Group 1.
Riddle, riddle, riddle Ree, | Do what I do after me; | Stamp, Clap, stamp, clap;

(Group 2.)
Riddle, riddle, riddle Ree, | Do what I do after me;

Sway - -, sway - - ; | Touch your toes, touch your nose; | Round in a circle

Stamp, Clap, stamp, clap; | Sway - -, sway - - ; | Touch your toes,

each one goes; | Bow once - -, Bow twice - -; | Bend down low and plant some

touch your nose; | Round in a circle each one goes; | Bow once - - -, Bow twice -

rice; | Lift your hands up to the sky; | Shake them out as sunbeams die;

- - -; | Bend down low and plant some rice; | Lift your hands up to the sky;

Clap your hands, Stamp your feet; | Cymbals clash and that's complete !

Shake them out as sunbeams die; | Clap your hands, Stamp your feet;

Cymbals clash and that's complete !

Suggestions: Do the movements which go with the text. A 4-part canon can be done after the class has achieved success in the 2-part canon arrangement. It is well to have a leader for each group. Phrase the speaking musically with voice inflection.
This idea can also become a game in improvised canon by using the first two measures of speech as the introduction. From there on omit the speech and do only the rhythmic movement, incorporating new ideas. Children take turns leading; the class follows (a movement later), imitating the action of the leader (one measure later).

(See Series II, book, Music with Children for additional Rhythmic Speech Canons.)

"Rhythm Speech Canon with Movement" from Grace Nash, *Music with Children, Series I* (LaGrange, Illinois: Kitching Educational, 1965), p.34. Used by permission of Grace Nash.

232

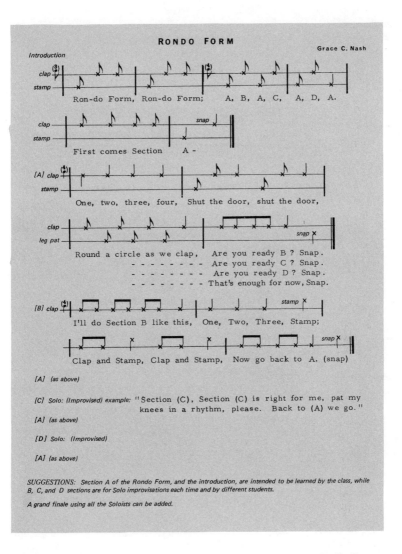

**RONDO FORM**

Grace C. Nash

*Introduction*

clap / stamp

Ron-do Form, Ron-do Form; A, B, A, C, A, D, A.

clap / stamp

First comes Section A -

[A] clap / stamp

One, two, three, four, Shut the door, shut the door,

clap / leg pat

Round a circle as we clap, Are you ready B ? Snap.
- - - - - - - - Are you ready C ? Snap.
- - - - - - - - Are you ready D ? Snap.
- - - - - - - - That's enough for now, Snap.

[B] clap

I'll do Section B like this, One, Two, Three, Stamp;

Clap and Stamp, Clap and Stamp, Now go back to A. (snap)

[A] *(as above)*

[C] *Solo: (Improvised) example:* "Section (C), Section (C) is right for me, pat my knees in a rhythm, please. Back to (A) we go."

[A] *(as above)*

[D] *Solo: (Improvised)*

[A] *(as above)*

*SUGGESTIONS: Section A of the Rondo Form, and the introduction, are intended to be learned by the class, while B, C, and D sections are for Solo improvisations each time and by different students.*

*A grand finale using all the Soloists can be added.*

"Rondo Form" from Grace Nash, *Music with Children, Series II* (LaGrange, Illinois: Kitching Educational, 1965), p.27. Used by permission of Grace Nash.

"Arkansas Traveler" from Grace Nash, *Chamber Music for Tonebar Instruments and Recorder* (LaGrange, Illinois: Kitching Educational, 1971), p.27. Used by permission of Grace Nash.

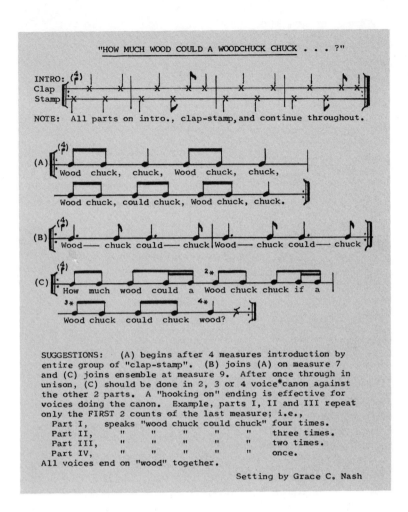

"HOW MUCH WOOD COULD A WOODCHUCK CHUCK . . . ?"

INTRO:
Clap
Stamp

NOTE: All parts on intro., clap-stamp, and continue throughout.

(A) Wood chuck, chuck, Wood chuck, chuck,
Wood chuck, could chuck, Wood chuck, chuck.

(B) Wood—— chuck could—— chuck |Wood—— chuck could—— chuck

(C) How much wood could a Wood chuck chuck if a
Wood chuck could chuck wood?

SUGGESTIONS: (A) begins after 4 measures introduction by entire group of "clap-stamp". (B) joins (A) on measure 7 and (C) joins ensemble at measure 9. After once through in unison, (C) should be done in 2, 3 or 4 voice*canon against the other 2 parts. A "hooking on" ending is effective for voices doing the canon. Example, parts I, II and III repeat only the FIRST 2 counts of the last measure; i.e.,

Part I,    speaks "wood chuck could chuck" four times.
Part II,      "      "      "      "      "      three times.
Part III,     "      "      "      "      "      two times.
Part IV,      "      "      "      "      "      once.
All voices end on "wood" together.

Setting by Grace C. Nash

"How Much Wood Could a Woodchuck Chuck . . . ?" from Grace Nash, *Music with Children: Rhythmic Speech Ensembles* (LaGrange, Illinois: Kitching Educational, 1966), p.13. Used by permission of Grace Nash.

235

Saying: "THE WORST WHEEL OF THE CART MAKES THE MOST NOISE"

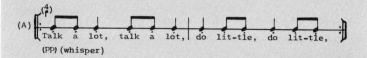

(A)

Talk a lot, talk a lot, do lit-tle, do lit-tle,

(PP) (whisper)

(B)

Yak-i-ty, yak-i-ty, yak-i-ty yak, chugga lugga, chugga lugga,

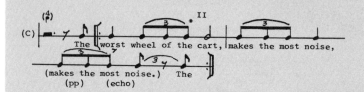

(C)

The worst wheel of the cart, makes the most noise,

(makes the most noise.) The

(pp) (echo)

Part (A) begins with a 2 measure introduction and Part (B) enters on measure 3. Part (C) enters on measure 5 and goes through once in unison, then 2 or 4 times in 2 part canon.

SUGGESTIONS: Part (A) speak very staccato except for the word "do". Introduction begins in a crisp whisper, gradually increasing dynamics to end of canon. On the last 2 measures of piece, Part (A) can divide into 2 groups, one taking the words "talk a", and the other taking the word "little". Speaking together, carry this for 2 measures and on the 4th beat of the 2nd measure both groups speak the word "nothing" loud.

Setting by Grace C. Nash

"The Worst Wheel of the Cart Makes the Most Noise," from Grace Nash, *Music with Children: Rhythmic Speech Ensembles* (LaGrange, Illinois: Kitching Educational, 1966), p.23. Used by permission of Grace Nash.

Courtesy Ludwig Drum Company, Chicago.

Establish the beat, showing arm signals alternately for *sol* and *la* (*S L S L*, etc.). Invite children to join in, keeping the same beat; then sing the song for them.

Now you sing the song with me.
Begin when all the children have the beat. Teach the Closet Key Game when the children have learned the song.

### Closet Key Game

Children form a circle and pass a large key (made of cardboard or similar material) around the circle while performing the arm signals on the beat. The key passes from hand to hand on each *la* arm signal. The child holding the key at the end of the first verse holds it up and sings "I found the closet key" to the tune of the song. Begin at a slow tempo.

▶ Turn to the chart.

Let's play our echo game with this song.
Echo-sing each line, using rhythm syllables, then tone syllables.

Which is higher, *sol* or *la*?
*La*

Is it very much higher, or right next door?
*Sol and la are next-door neighbors.*

*Sol* is around a line in this song. Where is *la*?
*In the space above sol*

Suppose *sol* were in a space. Where would *la* be then?
*Around the line above it*

*La* is always different. If *sol* is in a space, *la* is around a line. If *sol* is around a line, *la* is in a space; but they are always next to each other.

Sing the song again, this time with tone syllables, while I point to the notes. Use hand signals.

### MORE ACTIVITIES FOR CHILDREN

The teacher places the following exercise on the chalkboard and children fill in the *la*'s.

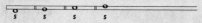

S        S        S        S

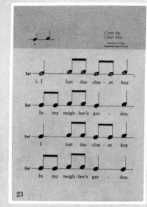

# I Lost the
# Closet Key

238

In this song, each of our fingers does a little dance.
Sing the first verse, tapping the beat with the thumb. On the line "So dance, my merry men, with him," all five fingers join in tapping the beat.

Each of my other fingers can "sing" the song, too. Join in with me when you are ready.
Continue until Pointer, Long Man, Ring Man, and Pinky have all danced. The children should be able to learn the song easily by imitation. When they have learned it, turn to the chart.

Clap the rhythm pattern. How many times do we clap the first line?
*Two times*

How do we know that?
*There is a repeat sign.*

When we sang the song before, did our fingers move to the beat, or to the rhythm?
*The beat*

Can you make your fingers dance to the rhythm this time?
Encourage the children to distinguish between tapping the beat and tapping the rhythm by lifting fingers on the rests.

Turn to "I Lost the Closet Key."

Where is *sol* in this song?
*Around a line*

# Dance, Thumbkin, Dance!

Where is *sol* in "Dance, Thumbkin, Dance!"?
*In a space*

Then where is *la*?
*Around a line*

Review the rule for the placement of *sol* and *la;* then all sing the song with tone syllables.

### MORE ACTIVITIES FOR CHILDREN

1. Vary the finger game by substituting a child's name for each finger. The child named goes to the center of the circle and creates his own dance. The other children imitate his dance on the line "So dance, my merry men, with him."
2. Sing "I Lost the Closet Key" and "Dance, Thumbkin, Dance!" substituting the word "line" and "space" for the tone syllables. The phrase "Dance, Thumbkin, dance" then becomes "Line, space, space, line" (| ⌐⌐ |).
 L   S   S   L

---

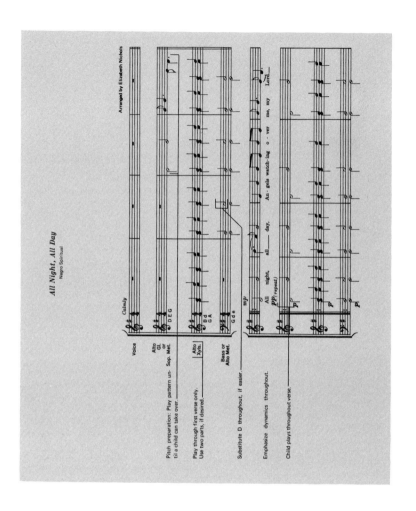

*All Night, All Day*

Negro Spiritual

Arranged by Elizabeth Nichols

240

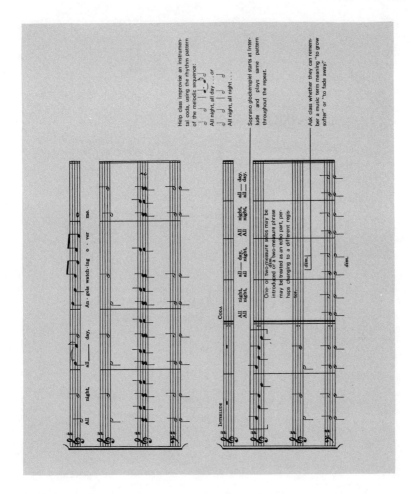

"All Night, All Day" from Elizabeth Nichols, *Orff Instrument Source Book,*
*Volume 1*, pp.10-11 © 1970 General Learning Corporation. Reprinted by permission.

241

## Git Along, Little Dogies
Cowboy Song

Song may be introduced by reading "The Cowboy's Life" (*Making Music Your Own*, 4), adding interpretive sounds and dramatizing the words.

Give special attention to the rhythm pattern by having class first speak the words against a six-beat meter, which may be set with body instruments.

Ask class which instrument part represents the jingling spurs.

Have players work out their own mallet technique according to their individual ability.

Pitch preparation

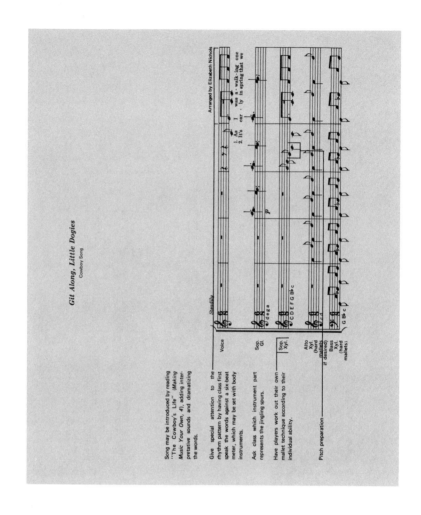

Arranged by Elizabeth Nichols

242

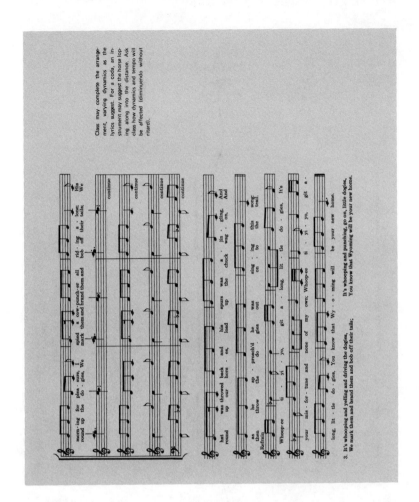

"Git Along, Little Dogies" from Elizabeth Nichols, *Orff Instrument Source Book, Volume 2*, pp.2-3 © 1971 General Learning Corp. Reprinted by permission.

inside yourself. [Pause.] Now let's read aloud the sounds these pictures are making and make the sounds exactly with that beat you have inside yourself."

As you move your finger under the pictures, the children will almost *sing*—tick-tock, tick-tock, swing-swing, swing-swing, jump-jump, jump-jump. Do not lose a beat between pictures.

Comment on how you liked the way the children changed their voices to suit the picture and the sound, for this is a very important point. In all music reading, the ability to change the mood of the sound is as important as pitch, tone, and rhythm. To keep the interest of the class high, move on to Chart 2 without too many repetitions.

## CHART 2

Chart 2 is read as "clap, clap, clap," etc. Ask the children to use their voices in a musical manner to make the clapping sounds sing. Have them clap as they speak the beat.

Point to the figure with outstretched arms. "Now," you say, "here is a silent beat. When we get there, throw your hands out like this [make a rest motion as illustrated on the chart] and throw away the sound. We will still feel the beat, but there is no sound. So keep your voices going and your hands clapping. Follow the pictures with my finger."

Go through the chart from the beginning and stop to look surprised if someone says "clap" where there is a silent beat. On the silent beat, *everyone* must be silent. This is a very important point. The silent beat must receive its full time, but no more than that. Do not hesitate after making the rest motion; move right on to the next beat.

After the children understand the silent beat, introduce them to the rest symbol, which follows quite naturally on the chart. Tell them that in music this symbol is called a *rest*. Emphasize, however, that it means to "throw away" the sound and not "to sit back and relax."

From Mary Helen Richards, *Threshold to Music, Primary Book* (Belmont, California: Fearon Publishers, 1964), p.14, chart 2. Used by permission.

# UNIT SEVEN

## The La Pentatonic Scale

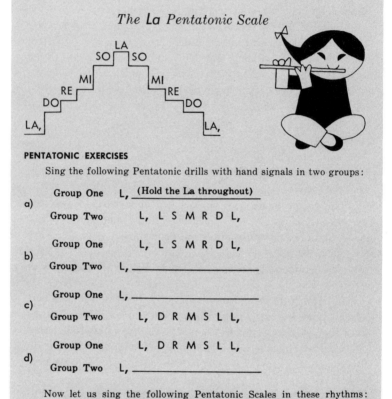

**PENTATONIC EXERCISES**

Sing the following Pentatonic drills with hand signals in two groups:

a)
| Group One | L, (Hold the La throughout) |
|---|---|
| Group Two | L, L S M R D L, |

b)
| Group One | L, L S M R D L, |
|---|---|
| Group Two | L, _____ |

c)
| Group One | L, _____ |
|---|---|
| Group Two | L, D R M S L L, |

d)
| Group One | L, D R M S L L, |
|---|---|
| Group Two | L, _____ |

Now let us sing the following Pentatonic Scales in these rhythms:

e) 2 | ⊓ | ⊓ ⊓ | l ⊓ | d ‖
　 L　S M R D L, D R　M S　L

f) 2 | l | ⊓ ⊓ | ⊓ ⊓ | l 𝄾 ‖
　 L, D R M S L S M R D L,

The La Pentatonic Scale" from Arpad Darazs and Stephen Jay, *Sight and Sound, Student Book* (New York: Boosey & Hawkes, Inc. 1965), p.37. Used by permission.

246

## ROTE SONG

Teach the new song, "What's Your Name?" (refer to Students' Manual, page 8). This is the first song in the Students' Manual.

### "WHAT'S YOUR NAME?"

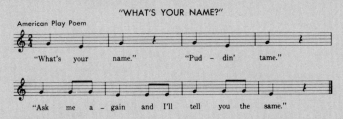

American Play Poem

"What's    your    name."        "Pud - din'    tame."

"Ask    me    a - gain    and    I'll    tell    you    the    same."

1. The teacher should encourage the students to listen for the rise and fall of the melody. The first three words are enough to convey the idea:

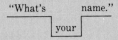

"What's    name."
your

2. The two sounds which are used in this song can be easily remembered because so many other songs also begin with the same two tones. For example, the class can sing the starting tones of "America The Beautiful" and be reminded that the entire song, "What's Your Name?" is made up of these two sounds.
3. Identify the upper tone as a sound called So and the lower tone as a sound called **Mi**. As the class sings "What's Your Name?" again, substitute the appropriate So or Mi for the words:

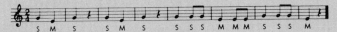

S    M    S        S    M    S        S    S    S    M    M    M    S    S    S    M

4. Present the hand signals as a way we can "show" the melody with our hands. The teacher should hold the hand at chest level for the So and move the hand several inches lower for the **Mi**.

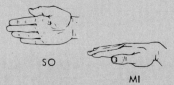

SO

MI

5. The students now sing "What's Your Name?" as they also make the hand signals. Their book illustrates how this should be done.
6. Encourage the class to supply the names of additional songs which begin with **So-Mi**, such as:

"Come Thou Almighty King" — first two tones

"Where Is My Little Dog Gone" — first three tones

"The Army Goes Rolling Along" — first nine tones